Intentional Communication:

Emotional Validation, Listening, Empathy, and the Art of Harmonious Relationships

By Patrick King
Social Interaction and Conversation Coach at
www.PatrickKingConsulting.com

Table of Contents

CHAPTER 4: HOW TO OWN YOUR EMOTIONS 133

Chapter 1: The Biggest Obstacle to Real Communication

"Deep human connection is the purpose and the result of a meaningful life—and it will inspire the most amazing acts of love, generosity and humanity."
- Melinda Gates

Each of us shares this planet with 7.8 billion other people. Let that sink in for a moment— 7.8 billion people, all unique, all playing out from birth to death and epic saga filled with love, fear, change, adversity, hope . . . just like you. A handful of people in that 7.8 billion are those who you love and cherish. But there are also the people you will work with and for, the people who can help you excel and achieve, the people who need your help and your unique gifts, and the people to challenge you to evolve in ways you can't yet imagine.

Despite our being jam-packed and full of possibilities to connect, the world today configured to reinforce an illusion of separateness. We may feel we are alone in our experience, with our sole responsibility being to advance our narrow interests, gain material security, or bolster our egos against a hostile and uninterested universe. And yet . . . in our most vulnerable moments, we remember what *really* matters: deep human connection.

If just one skill will guarantee you a happier, more successful life, it's the ability to have compassionate, cooperative relationships with other people. Whether it's with your family members, friends, colleagues, or romantic partners, no area of life isn't improved when you get on better with the other humans in your world. Poor relationships are arguably the most significant public health risk. Without proper communication, we cannot parent, unable to love, unable to lead in business, unable to negotiate, and entirely unable to make sense of our lives in our friendships, our families, our communities. Communication is nothing less than the fabric that stitches all 7.8 billion of us together.

In this book, we'll be looking at practical ways to transform yourself into someone likeable, who communicates well, and has meaningful, productive connections with others. Though this might be an area of difficulty for you currently, fortunately, we all have the capacity to improve the way we connect and communicate.

You versus Me . . . or Us versus the Problem

However, let's begin with all the things that stand in the way of us being the compassionate, emotionally intelligent people we want to be. If people desire better relationships, then why do they find it so difficult to cultivate them? Unfortunately, our world is geared up to emphasize the narcissistic, the competitive, and the combative in us, while there is comparatively little training or education on how to engage cooperatively with our fellow man. The first step to learning to be better is acknowledging what isn't working.

In this book, we'll keep returning to several core concepts and mindset shifts that underpin our approach to improving relationships. Perhaps the biggest one is simple: it's how we frame arguments.

Imagine a married couple who have precisely the same argument every few months. The wife feels emotionally neglected and sidelined while the husband works, and her fears mount until she raises the issue. She says, "I feel unloved," and he hears, "You don't love me. You're doing something wrong." He goes on the defensive and explains how hard he works—to support *her*! Isn't she grateful? Does she think that she's perfect? The wife feels even more unloved.

There are countless examples of these tiresome old arguments a million times worldwide. You've probably had some yourself, right? They all have in common is that they position the other person as an *enemy*. It's them versus you. Many of us go into combat mode so automatically that we literally cannot think of any other way to communicate. If you disagree, doesn't that logically make the other person your adversary?

The answer is no! Communication experts understand this point: That it's always you and the other person as a team working against the problem, rather than you and the other person working against one another. The goal of conversations is never to declare a winner. It's to create harmony, connection, and understanding. Imagine it as partner dancing rather than martial arts!

Simply get into the habit of saying, "We're on the same team," and you'll find this instantly brings you both into a more cooperative mindset. When you have a relationship with someone, healthy communication is geared toward protecting and maintaining that connection—not hurting the other person, blaming them, or discovering who is the villain and hero. This latter approach is like doing salsa dance with someone and trying to compete to see who can get to the end of the song fastest—not only does it not make sense, nobody will enjoy the experience!

Disagreement or conflict need not be an invitation to go into war mode with another person. The couple above can start to shift the issue when they realize that they love one another and are both on the same side. The wife loves her husband and wants to spend time with him; the husband loves his wife and wants to provide for her. When they stop seeing one another as the source of the problem, they can appreciate this monumental fact and put it front and center.

No offense and defense, but teamwork.
No blame or guilt, but honest identification of the problem, and a joint effort to fix it.
No you and me, but us.
Your enemy is not the other person, but whatever is standing in the way of your connection.
No winner and loser; we win together, or we lose together.

Often, people get into heated arguments because deep down, they feel threatened, unloved, unheard, or disrespected. These needs can be so strong and overpowering that they temporarily eclipse the need for relationship harmony. Here, we make a mistake: this zero-sum thinking has us believing that either we get what we want, **or** the other person gets what they want. So, if we feel like we are not getting enough understanding or love, we assume we have to take it from the other person. If we want to feel right, we assume that we need to make the other person feel wrong.

In a healthy relationship of any kind, goodwill, love, and respect are not finite quantities that have to be squabbled over. Everyone can be right! Or two people can differ in their opinions, yet there is no problem and no reason to fight.

An emotional discussion often has a feeling of lack or fear at its very core. When you say, "We're a team," it helps dissolve these feelings and orient you toward solutions. In mentioning solutions, however, there are two levels that conversations of this kind usually play out on:

1. **The objective content**
2. **The emotional content**

Imagine a friend shows up late to a meeting, and the other friend is angry about it. They argue. The objective content is the fact of the tardiness, and they may fight at length about exactly why the friend was late, and the times it's happened before, and how bad lateness is or isn't. But while the argument is a tussle between the friends over where to assign blame, the emotional content is going unspoken: one friend is hurt that the other does not value their friendship as much as they do. Some relationships are one hundred percent objective content—they keep returning to the petty details because they never address the real emotional core of the problem.

The next time you argue with someone, take a pause and ask yourself grounding questions:

- Are you trying to protect and deepen your connection, or are you trying to prove that you're the winner, i.e., you're right and they're wrong?

- Have you unconsciously (or consciously!) positioned the other person up as an attacker or enemy?
- Are you exclusively focused on your viewpoint and forcing the other person to accept it rather than seeking a compromise between you?
- What is the emotional content of the situation right now?

Arguments are a natural part of life. We can navigate them in such a way as to create distance and fear, or we can use them as opportunities to grow as individuals and strengthen our bonds with others.

In the thick of an argument, it's tempting to enjoy being the victim, to heap blame on others, to shut down in defensiveness, or to get aggressive. Even if you "win" an argument this way, though, you ultimately lose. It's essential to learn of your emotions and see that no matter how strong or unpleasant they are, it doesn't change that you and the other person are a solid, unified team.

If you're struggling, turn your attention away from the other person and look at yourself for a moment. Ask what is stopping you from seeing the other person as an ally and partner. Dig deep, and you'll likely find unmet needs. In later chapters, we'll talk about ways to get these needs met *without* making the other person responsible or wrong. But for now, it's enough to simply remind yourself that disagreement, friction, hurt, or confusion are normal. The good news? We can disagree with someone and *still have a good relationship with them*. We can still listen, we can still be heard, and we can still communicate with compassion and respect.

The goal of all communication is to maintain a healthy and happy connection.
The goal is not to beat the other person down, win, make your case, blame them, get them to recognize your truth, or feel vindication for achieving the higher ground.

Tune all your awareness to the former goal, and arguments will cease to be a threat to your relationships.

Assume People are Doing Their Best

Closely connected to this mindset shift is the ability to "assume noble intent." The trigger for going into war mode is to assume that you are under attack. Like the husband in our example, you hear a threat and an accusation where there isn't one. You respond to the threat you think you hear rather than the real person in front of you and the emotional content they are trying to communicate. This sets up a conversation where your defensive ego is warring against the other person's defensive ego. While the worst parts of yourselves are in vicious battle, the more vulnerable, genuine parts are cowering in the background unacknowledged.

Assuming noble intent goes beyond giving people the benefit of the doubt . . . although many relationships would drastically improve if people did only that! Consciously be a person who approaches any interaction with another human in a spirit of fairness and kind-heartedness. Today, the media constantly bombards people with visions of fear and hatred. They may feel that the world is hostile, ugly, and their baseline attitude is mistrust. It can be an act of principled bravery to nevertheless see the good in others and lead with honest and noble intentions anyway.

Assuming noble intent is a way of applying one's own higher moral values to one's own behavior. When you carry yourself with dignity, honesty, and kindness, you naturally expect it in others and can inspire it in return, creating a domino effect of opportunity—the opportunity to be a good human who works in harmony with other similarly intentioned humans.

Rather than seeing kindness as something people need to earn, coax out, or win from you, you are generous in spirit and begin with kindness as a default. You have a perspective that invited others to show up as their best selves. With such open-mindedness, you communicate trust and goodwill to others, open lines of communication, and invite them to engage with you as one worthy peer to another. Yes, we can all view one another as enemies—

but why not lead by expecting better from yourself and from them?

If you feel bitter about humanity, or mistrustful of others, try reminding yourself that people are generally good. Yes, really! When they're bad, they are so from ignorance, fear, or misunderstanding, or because they lack insight into the consequences of their choices. But we can view the errors of others with compassion and forgiveness, or even with a commitment to understanding them rather than condemning them. Again, this is ennobling for *us* as much as it is for them!

When you assume that people are doing the best they can with the available resources (inner and outer), you free yourself from the stress and burden of judging them, and you allow yourself to connect more deeply with them or find solutions.

Assume that *you* are fundamentally good, too. It's easier to see the noble intent in others when we recognize and exalt it in ourselves. We develop self-esteem and dignity simultaneously as we give our trust and beneficence to others. No matter the issue or problem at hand, assuming noble intent will ensure you're getting the most from any communication.

No, you don't have to be gullible or a pushover. But you empower yourself with your own principles and put them front and center. Lead by example. Assume that others are good by default, right from the start, not because you have evidence for that conclusion, but because this perspective is the fastest and easiest way to understanding and collaboration. It can instantly dissolve hurt and misunderstanding. Adopt this attitude, and you may be pleasantly surprised at the nobleness you inspire in others—people *want* to be good. They want to give you what you want. Isn't it a relief to go about your business believing this is the case?

We've seen how assuming people are enemies is a foolproof way to damage relationships. Assuming noble intent is the opposite, like fertilizer for growing respectful relationships. Believe that other people's actions (even their irritating, confusing, or downright awful ones) come ultimately from a place of goodness. Assume people have good characters and want to live by their values. Choose to forego making everyone your adversity and invite them to be better than that. After all, we all have hearts and souls, we all yearn for a higher purpose, we all hurt and feel vulnerable, and we're all trying our best with the tools we have right now.

People don't always have *positive* intent. You may not understand their values or agree with them from your own perspective. But try to understand their actions through their lens. Assume that their behavior makes sense to them, if only you could gain insight into the rules that govern their world. It's very easy to assume other people are just jerks. But it's lazy, and it's never true. Think about all the regrettable actions you've taken in the past—in your own way, didn't you have a reason? Didn't you deserve compassion and understanding? Even if you acted completely appallingly, it doesn't negate that you are a human with hopes and fears and the desire to be better.

Assume that other people are just like you! People are not always angels, and some people do act malevolently. But if we turn up to any conversation or interaction with a readiness and willingness to perceive the intrinsic good in people, we are priming ourselves (and them!) to let our higher values guide us.

Let's say your mother-in-law gives you a children's book for your birthday. You're insulted—it's a silly kid's story meant for ten-year-olds; does she think you're an idiot? If you assume noble intent, you talk to her further and realize she bought the gift because she remembers a story about your childhood and thought the book would be a cute bit of nostalgia for you. Now, she's wrong about this and misunderstood your childhood anecdote. But if you can look past this is and see her noble intent, all friction and mistrust dissolve.

If a driver cuts you off on the road, you can shrug and assume noble intent. Maybe they're having a bad day. Maybe they're a teenager, and their higher brain hasn't finished maturing yet! Maybe it was a simple accident, and they didn't maliciously plan to hurt you on purpose.

People do the best they can with the tools they have available. Think back to yourself ten or twenty years ago and how you solved certain problems or approached certain relationships. Chances are, you'd do things differently now because you know better. Deep compassion comes when you realize that the "bad people" you encounter in life are just good people temporarily acting out a bad role at the moment. We had awful tantrums when we were two because we weren't emotionally mature. We said regrettable things in the heat of the moment because we were triggered and lashing out in fear. We made the choice we did because we weren't aware of other choices we could have made.

But we grew up and stopped having tantrums, we apologized for lashing out when we calmed down, and we made better choices as we learned of them. Reminding yourself of this phenomenon in others makes relationships so much calmer and kinder. When you're face to face with someone doing something you hate or disagree with, or when someone is hurting you, remember that you are not seeing *all* of who they are. You can respond to the negativity you see in the moment, or you can trust that they have a kinder, more rational and calmer self hiding in there.

Well, what happens if you are serene and magnanimous and assume noble intent in someone who consistently shows you that they're a complete jerk? Well, *you* can rest assured that you've done your best. Take a breath, step away for a while, and get perspective. You are never responsible for what other people choose. But you will always feel better about yourself if you know in your heart that you have given other people ample opportunity to meet you halfway. Who said you have to convince anyone, anyway? If you've assumed noble intent, it's easy to walk away from damaging or negative people with a light heart and a clean conscience.

Telling the Third Story

Letting go of your ego in interactions with others is easier said than done, but it is the quickest way to restore harmony. When crusading for your own viewpoint and valiantly battling everyone until you strong-arm them into agreeing with you, you forget one crucial detail: you might be wrong. And worse than that, you could be mistaken in the belief that you can frame the situation as right and wrong in the first place!

Basically, clinging to your perspective and wanting to broadcast it as The One True Way gives you serious tunnel vision. It shuts you off to the reality. . . a reality that inconveniently contains everyone else and all their thoughts and beliefs. Whenever there is more than one person, there will be more than one reality. And that's just fine.

Now, we should be careful here—we're not saying that personal feelings trump objective reality and plain facts. But we are saying that in arguments or disagreements, it's seldom about plain facts. Rather, every person's reality contains their perspective, values, unique past experiences, personal identity, particular narrative on the issue at hand, and the outcome they most want. This is more akin to the emotional content of communication than the objective content (i.e., facts).

As the saying goes, there are always three stories in any argument—yours, mine, and the truth. Though this is simplifying it, the idea is sound. In no interaction is any single person one hundred percent "correct." You simply cannot think this way. If you read that sentence and think, "Well, what about those crazy flat-earthers? They believe something that's patently false. In an argument with them, I know I'd be one hundred percent right."

First, this observation perhaps explains why flat-earthers get as much media exposure as they do—people love to feel superior to them! Second, if we remember the difference between objective content and emotional content, we will see that even this example is not as cut and dried as it seems. If someone says, "The earth is flat," then you might respond, "no it isn't, what a moronic thing to say." But what if someone said, "I'm overwhelmed and frightened by the complexity of the world, and I feel distrustful of a government that has demonstrably led me astray for profit. I know I sound nutty, but conspiracy theories give me a sense of control over the world. I hate how reductive and dehumanizing science can be, and how pompous scientists are, and in going against them, I feel like I restore some of my own humanity and agency. Plus, my parents constantly undermined and devalued me as a child, and that's why today I have a vehement need to assert myself and not be told to shut up or that I'm stupid." How would you respond to *that*?

In any interaction, nobody has an exclusive right to "the truth." Nobody may claim to be a perfectly neutral arbiter of reality (which, incidentally, is what many people think they are accessing when they claim to be "on the side of science"). Each of us has our own biases, expectations, past experiences, beliefs, and perspectives. Each of us colors our interactions with our feeling tone, personality, style of communication, and values and priorities. None of this is ever neutral. And in this specificity, we are all equal.

Whether we agree or not on superficial facts or data is irrelevant (after all, how often do "facts" actually change?). These superficial details are in the realm of ego and conflict. If we go beyond this realm, we can do something better than compete with others—we can *understand* them. Approaching conversations this way takes courage and honesty. Many of us unconsciously believe that we are the center of the universe and that what we think is obviously the best and only way to think, or that it's only our perspective that ultimately matters.

One amazing way to counteract this short sightedness is the "third story" approach. Imagine a third, neutral observer watching the situation unfold next time you're in a conflict. Now, imagine how they would relate the narrative—i.e., the "third story" they'd tell. Look at all three stories and become curious about the differences between them.

See if you can agree with the other person on this third story. This is where the magic happens, as it can put you on the path to mutual understanding and compromise. The third story becomes an anchor or a shared reality that both people can hold on to even as they inhabit their different perspectives.

For example, a couple is planning a wedding. One of them spends money immediately, saying he only plans to get married once and he intends to do it in style. No expense is spared. The other is freaked out at the prospect of spending so much money, and she's petrified of starting her married life in debt. They both argue more and more until a big blow out over the exorbitant cost of a four-tier chocolate fountain.

His story: Weddings are joyful occasions, and a chance to show your family a good time and boast a little to your friends you can afford the luxury. Love and commitment in the relationship are proportionate to the money spent. Basically, stinginess = the couple isn't really in love.

Her story: Weddings are solemn, meaningful occasions about commitment and intimacy. They're a time to demonstrate your values to others. Spending a lot of money on a wedding is vulgar and financially unwise. Couples who splash money around come across as insincere and materialistic—they must be compensating for a lack of true love!

Well, what about the third story?

Third story: They each have different understandings of what weddings mean and their function. They each have different beliefs and feelings about spending money. When money is spent, he feels glad, but she feels anxious. The difference leads to arguments.

Isn't that so much more . . . relaxed? Seeing things this way, they can see that the problem is their different expectations of a wedding. The problem is not that she's wrong or that he's wrong. If they can keep returning to the third story, they locate the real root of the trouble and give themselves a chance to solve it rather than going round in circles about this bill or that bill. Now, they have a real chance of finding a compromise.

They can both identify their deeper needs and seek to make sure they *both* have those needs met, with as little conflict as possible. Again, it's us versus the problem. Granted, they may not magically make all the tension disappear. And after a while, they may discover that their differences are not reconcilable. Using the third-story trick cannot magically erase all differences and frictions, but it can help you get an honest handle on them and give you the best chance of compromise—which you don't get at all when you're each just arguing your own perspective.

Address the Higher Self, Acknowledge the Emotional Self

When you frame problems as something you mutually solve as a team, when you assume people are doing their best and when you actively seek to find commonality in a third story, you are operating at a different level than if you merely butt heads with the other person on who's version of reality is the winning one. You're operating at a level that prioritizes connection above ego.

Consistently do this, and you will discover just how easy it is to meet everyone's needs.

So many people get into arguments because they unconsciously fear that "compromise" and cooperation means loss. They may feel that if they are accommodating, kind, and compassionate, they'll be taken advantage of, won't get their needs met, or will lose out. In fact, the opposite is true—people who are open-minded, respectful, curious about mutual solutions, and kind are far more likely to get what they want and need in any situation.

Sadly, it's all too common for people to communicate from a position of fear and insecurity. This puts them on the defensive, makes them assume the worst of others, and even go into attack because they believe they are protecting themselves. This then triggers other people's defenses. The problem is not only unsolved, but also worsened.

Instead, we can proactively take the position of tuning into the emotional content of what people are saying, whether they can responsibly communicate that or not. You have two choices: you can speak to their higher, more noble self, or you can talk directly to their fears, their biases, and, to be frank, the worst parts. Here's a hint: doing this will bring the worst out in *you*.

The Buddhist "namaste" greeting embodies the former idea nicely—we say to another person, "the Buddha in me recognizes the Buddha in you." No matter how hostile or difficult someone is, try to remember that they have a beautiful, amazing, and inspiring self within them. Try to remember that they have wonderful qualities, that they have the potential for greatness, and that inside them, they can love and suffer, just like you. Talk to *that* version of them.

Imagining that other people are flat, boring caricatures and not nuanced and complex beings is a) easier and b) usually makes us feel better about ourselves. We imagine that we are the main protagonists in our lives, with full and rich inner worlds, and others are just "non-player characters" who are not as essential or multifaceted as we are. Everyone else is the center of their own universe. They feel about themselves how you feel about yourself . . . and *you* are just the supporting actor in *their* main story!

Some people find it elevates your perspective to remember that the person before you used to be an innocent child once. They were young, hopeful and playful. They had a best friend, feared the dark, and wore a woolly jumper with yellow ducks on it. Just like you, they had their first love and their first big disappointment. Just like you, they lay awake nights worried about it all. Just like you, they have insecurities and deep secrets they've told no one. They cry when they're hurt. They've shown touching acts of kindness to others. They have dreams. Talents. Questions. Dazzlingly unique insights and opinions. Everything.

Having "compassion" is sometimes reduced to a bland tolerance of people we don't like but have to bear with. But why limit yourself to mere tolerance? People are *wonderful*. They are works of art. Their perspectives, feelings, and desires are not just something to begrudgingly accommodate to get along, but something to celebrate, learn about, lovingly accept, and welcome. When you stop seeing difference as a threat or a problem, you can appreciate it as a fascinating source of enrichment in life.

But what does addressing someone's higher self look like? For one, it's assuming the best of others and generously giving the benefit of the doubt, as we've seen. It's also the willingness to imagine, on faith, that people are good, that people make sense, and that people want to help you and engage in mutually satisfying relationships.

It means treating people with respect and trust even when they have difficulty respecting or trusting themselves, and even if they've done little to earn it! A manager at work may approach his team with the deep belief that each has something unique and valuable to offer. Instead of micromanaging them, he tells them, "I hired you because you're good at what you do. How about you just run with this project and see what happens? I trust you to make the right decision." It's hard to imagine an employee not feeling respected and valued when told that.

Or imagine a parent who has a teenager who's gotten into trouble at school. Instead of launching into a shame-heavy lecture about what they should have done and how disappointed everyone is, the parent could say, "You know what, you're old enough know to know right from wrong. You're a smart person, and I know you're also kind. What do *you* think about what you've done? I wonder if you feel that this is the kind of thing that reflects your values, or if you want to try and do something better?"

Doing this, the parent is communicating a few things: that they know and trust that the teenager has values, these are worth exploring and committing to, and that the parent will not impose their values, but give the teenager space to figure out on their own. Again, the result is likely to be a heightened feeling of respect, empathy and responsibility. Instead of addressing the bad in their character, they address the good and use that as a point of departure.

In a couple's argument, one spouse is offended that the other forgot their birthday. But in love, they address their higher nature.

They say, "I know you care about me. I'm sure you didn't mean to hurt me, but you forgot my birthday. Why?" This is not placing blame. It's not making assumptions or going on the offense. It's simply taking the highest nature of the other person as a given and leading with curious respect. It's seeking to understand the problem rather than going in with guns blazing. "She forgot my birthday, and she did it because she's selfish and doesn't give a damn about me."

If you're feeling angry and attacked yourself, it's challenging to assume the best of people. But this is when you most need to try! Instead of getting carried away in strong emotions, gain perspective by acknowledging their most vulnerable self. When you're face to face with someone being difficult or annoying or mean, it's easy to forget that they have a vulnerable self— but they do.

A core of non-violent communication (more on this later) is to focus on people's needs in any exchange. People communicate (even badly) because they want to meet their needs. They sometimes succeed and often don't, but this is ultimately what's behind all communication, including aggression, stubbornness, fear, and criticism.

So, when you're with a difficult person or in a challenging or unpleasant situation, ask yourself:

What are my needs here, and how can I communicate them clearly to others?
What are their needs, and how can I help them achieve those needs?

That's it. Don't waste too much time on anger, fear, or red herring details. If someone is being judgmental of you, examine the situation closely—you may discover that their criticism stems from a deep insecurity in themselves. They may feel worthless and judge others to meet a certain need, i.e., to feel better about themselves. This insight alone can help you defuse situations with them . . . as well as know not to take their judgment personally!

Mastering Self-Differentiation

We'll consider one final mindset: the ability to self-differentiate, which is a concept few are familiar with. It's the capacity to separate your thoughts from your feelings, and separate your thoughts and feelings from other people's. If you've ever had trouble thinking because you feel flooded with emotions, you were experiencing difficulty with differentiation. If someone ties up their opinions and beliefs with others' or cannot decide what they think and feel without consulting others, it also signals a lack of self-differentiation.

Relating with other humans is a delicate dance—we are always separate, unique individuals, but we also mutually influence one another. Healthy connections occur when both parties are sufficiently self-differentiated yet still connected. All kinds of entanglement and "bleeding over" of identities, thoughts, and feelings occur when they're not. How do you know if you are properly and healthily differentiated in a relationship? Simple: ask yourself whether you can be different without losing emotional connection.

Connection based on sharing identical opinions and values means both parties are mutually defining one another rather than defining themselves first and *then* encountering one another as separate beings, with respect and curiosity. If we are differentiated, we can calmly reflect on any difference of opinion or conflict without jeopardizing the connection. If not, the difference will become a source of conflict or threaten the connection. When differentiated, we take responsibility for our own contribution, and recognize what "stuff" belongs to the other person. If not, we may be over- or under-responsible, enmeshed, or liable to confuse our thoughts and opinions with those of others.

The trick is always to maintain a *clear relationship with yourself.* For some people, relationships of any kind are always total and devouring—it's being themselves OR being in a relationship. To maintain a relationship where differences are contained comfortably, however, takes maturity and self-awareness. This is why an indicator of an undifferentiated relationship is all-or-nothing, my-way-or-the-highway thinking. If you are a rebel and choose the opposite of everyone else's opinions, don't be fooled into thinking you are well-differentiated—you are still basing your thoughts, feelings, and opinions concerning other people's.

Other examples of poor differentiation:

- Feeling smothered and controlled by a person's intrusive, dominating attitude.
- Being unable to say what you think or feel without checking the opinions of others first.
- In a relationship, if one person feels something, the other person cannot help feeling the same as well.
- Being unable to express a different opinion because of fear of causing offense or friction. Going along with whatever's happening and forfeiting one's own opinion.
- Seeing negative emotions in a person you love and feeling personally responsible. Even worse if the

unhappy person is ready to blame you!

- Having concerns, boundaries, or misgivings but feeling unable to speak out, or you do and are not heard.
- Feeling other people's emotions as your own . . . but being unsure of what you yourself feel.
- Any relationship where the unspoken rule is, "To be in this relationship, you cannot be your authentic self."

To improve your relationships, get into the habit of asking yourself, **what is my stuff, and what is theirs?**

Being authentic, self-defined, and conscious of your unique thoughts and feelings takes courage and honesty. What is *your* opinion, regardless of how others respond to it? What do *you* think is independent of the beliefs and worldviews of those around you?

Once you clarify this for yourself, you can do the next important step: **cultivate relationships that can tolerate normal differences in feeling and opinion.** Don't make complete agreement a condition of intimacy, and don't accept these terms from others who would rather engage with a copy of themselves than a unique person different from them.

One useful way to get better at this is to learn the difference between *observation* and *evaluation*, which we will explore in more detail in later chapters.

How to express difference (of thought or opinion) with others while still maintaining closeness with them is to use observations rather than judgments and evaluations. To explain the difference: "it's raining" is a neutral, objective observation, but "I can't believe it's this godawful drizzle again, I HATE IT!" is an evaluation and judgment.

If we approach communication with an attitude of evaluation, we are instigating defensiveness in the other person. We're making value judgments and indirectly positioning our perspective as right, whereas theirs is wrong and needs to change. Problems also occur when we state evaluations as though they are observations (i.e., positioning our opinions as facts) or mixing the two.

Teasing out what is observed and what is evaluation takes awareness and self-differentiation. When emotions are running high, things can get very confusing, and people can get hurt long before they realize what's happened and why. But just like the neutral observer who tells the "third story," we can use observations to ground us and reach a compromise and understanding.

We can ask ourselves what our business is and what the other person's is, but **what is objective fact and what is evaluation and opinion?**

This can help us avoid misunderstanding when we communicate with others, but also help us untangle other people's communications when they may be coming from a not-so-differentiated perspective. Let's return to our example of the couple with different ideas about weddings. She might say to her fiancé, "Why are you so obsessed with serving everyone real champagne? We can just serve them something cheaper. The world's not going to end just because you buy budget booze, you know."

If he is undifferentiated and triggered emotionally, he'll probably respond defensively to such a statement. But let's imagine he instead asks:

What is my stuff here, and what is hers?
What is fact, and what is opinion?

He can step back and realize that the idea that he is "obsessed" is not objective but her evaluation of his emotions. If he confidently and comfortably knows himself, he knows that he is *not* materialistic, obsessed, or petty. He knows that he is simply excited. If he only responds to the judgment dripping from her statements, things will escalate into an argument. But he could also remain differentiated and anchor himself in the objective. In his fiancé's world, caring about champagne is a little shallow and silly. But in his world, it's not. However, if he can stay within his own thoughts and feelings, he will not get triggered by her unkind remark and can assert boundaries, stand his ground, and seek to understand what she feels—without letting her dictate what *he* feels. And he can do all this without having the differences, which means that the relationship is doomed!

Takeaways:

- Everyone can learn to be better at communication, listening, and being heard. This can improve every kind of relationship, and help you deal with difficult people and conflict.
- Cultivating empathetic, meaningful, and genuine connections with others means being aware of the barriers to that connection and committing to removing them.
- One significant obstacle is the mindset that positions others as enemies or adversaries rather than collaborators on the same team. A healthier approach is "it's you and me versus the problem." Disagreement and difference are not necessarily a threat if both parties are dedicated to working together.

- Assume noble intent and that people are doing their best. This will put you in a proactive, generous, and optimistic frame of mind that will inspire the best from others and keep you open to solutions and possibilities. Be kind and seek the moral high ground just because!
- In conflict, try to imagine a neutral observer and the "third story" they'd tell so you can identify a set of facts about the situation that both parties can agree on. Harmonious relationships begin when we abandon our egoistic need to be right.
- In every interaction, consciously address the other person's highest self, or at least their most vulnerable and human self. Acknowledge emotional content and not just superficial details. Have compassion, awareness, and genuine curiosity for other people's different perspectives.
- Finally, master self-differentiation and be crystal clear on thoughts versus feelings, and your thoughts and feelings versus those of others. Defuse conflict by taking responsibility for your perspective while seeing the other person's for what it is. Most important, have the maturity to

maintain intimacy with others despite differences in opinion. Routinely ask what your "business" versus theirs is and what is observation versus evaluation.

Chapter 2: Real-World Skills for Better Communication

The last chapter explored the fundamental mindsets that underpin healthy, cooperative relationships with others. In this chapter, we're looking more closely at concrete skills to improve how you communicate with others. Think of communication as a way of expressing who you are, what you want, and your fundamental attitude to relationships. If we have an unhealthy attitude from the start, all communication will be unhealthy. That's why it's worth shifting our mindset before we embark on learning specific new communication skills.

The Gentle Power of Assertiveness

With self-differentiation, we've seen that we have the courage and confidence to stand our ground and own our unique perspectives, feelings, and thoughts without allowing ourselves to be swayed by others. This goes hand in hand with assertiveness.

We need a huge caveat, though. Being assertive is **not** about getting others to do what you want, agree with you, think or feel the same as you do, or shut up and listen to you! Assertiveness is something we do within ourselves for ourselves. It's an attitude that often expresses itself in words or actions, but it is firstly an attitude. When we understand our own needs, take responsibility for them and have enough presence of mind to transmit them honestly and respectfully to others, then we are assertive. If we want to control or dominate others, this is not assertiveness at all—it demonstrates a special insecurity and lack of power.

In relationships, we've seen that zero-sum thinking, viewing the other as an enemy and operating from fear and mistrust are recipes for disaster. We can unconsciously believe that we have to somehow force others to treat us well. We imagine that there's only so much love and affection to go around, and that if we want some, we have to wrestle it from others. Perhaps we believe that we have to be loud, powerful, or domineering for people to respect us. Or that we have to push to the front of the proverbial queue or be a little rude to stop others from walking all over us.

Genuine assertiveness and confidence look nothing like the stereotypes. The truly strong, confident, and self-assured person need not be a loud bully. They can be perfectly polite, relaxed, humorous, accommodating, and kind. All that's required is for them to know their needs and quietly yet firmly assert them. And it's "assert"—not shout, not demand, and certainly not beg or convince or manipulate. Simply assert with the same easy certainty as you would assert, "The sky is blue."

This goes back to self-differentiation. When we know ourselves and who we are, we don't get caught up in who others are. We like and respect who they are, but it has nothing to do with what we know and what we do for ourselves. Likewise, if we know our worth, we don't get caught up trying to force others to acknowledge it. If we know what we need, others can't tell us what they think we should have. And if we are deeply convinced of our own right to hold boundaries and have our (reasonable) needs met, then we don't get into scuffles and arguments over what we are and are not entitled to. Incidentally, when we are self-assertive, we find it much easier to grant other people their assertiveness, and we easily and happily respect their boundaries. Self-differentiation, confidence, respect, and assertively defended boundaries are all part and parcel of the same mindset.

Let's put this all into concrete, usable terms.

1. You are a human being who is no better and no worse than other human beings, and have innate worth. From this worth comes the entitlement to satisfy your own reasonable needs (not wants and desires but needs).

2. As a unique and self-differentiated individual, it's your responsibility to know your needs and communicate these to others with clarity and respect.
3. If you establish a healthy boundary that is disrespected, it's your responsibility to follow up with consequences or remove yourself from the situation.

Notice anything interesting about the above? None of it has anything to do with getting other people to do things. It's all about what *you* do. Being an assertive person with good boundaries is not about having rules for how other people treat you, but rules about how you're willing to be treated, given your own reasonable needs.

You cannot control what other people do, only what you do. You're responsible for knowing and communicating your needs, and they communicate and know theirs. This means you cannot be expected to read other people's minds, nor can you expect them to read yours—we all have to proactively and clearly *communicate* our needs to others. If we're in the territory of what other people should and shouldn't do, we are intruding into their territory. It is never for us to say what another person's life means, what they should value, how they should act, or the perspective they should take.

However, asking clearly and assertively for what you need isn't a guarantee that you'll get it. Let's be honest—life isn't fair. Sometimes good people are not given what they need, and sometimes being in the right doesn't spare you any injustice. Still, this doesn't absolve us from taking charge and asserting who we are, and what we need.

In any conversation, don't tell people what to do. Instead, tell them your needs. Listen to their needs. Put up a boundary according to your values and limits. If a boundary is repeatedly violated, don't get angry and hang around trying to manipulate the other person into caring or repenting—just leave and get your needs met elsewhere. You have a right to seek your needs, and they (frustratingly) have a right not to meet yours. But then again, you may walk away from such a person! It's all a matter of choices.

One easy way to develop healthy assertiveness in relationships is to watch out for the word "should." If you find yourself saying what the other person should be doing, pause and check in instead with what you need in that moment. To be heard? To be left alone? A little affection? Respect? Then say so. Turn the focus away from their actions and onto your own needs. So, instead of saying, "My job should be paying me more," empower yourself by saying, "I need a higher salary and more recognition." Now, you can choose what to do. Ask for a raise? Look for a better job? You're not stuck waiting for someone else to act before you can get your needs met. You are taking that action yourself.

But What About Empathy?

With all this talk about asserting boundaries and self-differentiating, you might have wondered—where does empathy feature?

Here's the thing: if you cultivate some mindsets already outlined and take responsibility for your own thoughts, feelings, and perspectives, you'll automatically have more empathy for others. Sometimes the assumption is that assertiveness = being mean, and that empathy = being nice (but a bit of a pushover). However, good interpersonal skills stem from *knowing and respecting ourselves*. The relationship we have with ourselves is reflected in our relationships with others, and vice versa.

Empathy is nothing more complicated than recognizing and acknowledging another person's lived reality, including their thoughts, feelings, and perspectives. It's the ability to see and accept their experience for what it is, even if it's different from our own. Sympathy is said to be knowing that someone is feeling something, but it contains no deep understanding of what they're experiencing.

There are types of empathy, too. **Cognitive empathy** is having insight into another person's experience, but this is a neutral, intellectual understanding and not an emotional one. A therapist, for example, might recognize the symptoms of post-natal depression in a client and have deep theoretical comprehension of what's going on without having personal experience with the issue.

Emotional empathy is understanding a person's experience on a deeper, felt level. Their feeling affects you and causes you to feel, too. While this empathy can create strong bonds and compassion, it can also be overwhelming and lead to people losing their self-differentiation. Also, having strong emotional empathy doesn't make you more able to help or solve a problem—in fact, deep feeling may incapacitate you as much as it does the other person!

Finally, so-called **compassionate empathy** is about the ability to take concrete steps to reduce the suffering you see in others. In a conversation, this could look like actively trying to reassure someone desperate for comfort or suggesting a practical solution for someone too overwhelmed to seek that solution themselves.

The above three types of empathy build on one another—cognitive empathy often leads to emotional empathy, which can then inspire us to do something helpful. In any situation, you can activate your empathy by remembering this hierarchy, and starting with cognitive empathy first.

<u>Step 1:</u> To cultivate cognitive empathy, play with switching viewpoints and perspectives and understand where the person is coming from, what they want, and why. Listen with full, non-judgmental attention and set aside your own assumptions or biases. You might need to listen to their verbal and nonverbal communication. Try to put words to their emotions and ask questions rather than assuming you know what they feel.

Simply seek to understand. Remind yourself that people always make sense on their own terms, and that they're trying the best they can to solve their needs—what are those needs? Don't interpret and theorize and come with evaluations. Just listen. You don't have to agree or see how their experience compares with yours. Just see what it feels like for them, in their world. For example, in a disagreement with a family member from a different generation, you might take the time to simply hear them out without going into defense mode or hurrying to explain your side of the story.

You can see intellectually that their interpretation of events differs from yours. You see the way they understand a shared event and the terms they use. You see why they feel as they do. You ask questions. Maybe you imagine you're David Attenborough in a documentary trying to understand their behavior like an anthropologist!

Step 2: Now, you can try to find emotional empathy. Cognitive empathy paves the way for this, but you can encourage it by actively imagining yourself in their position. Try to find points of common ground. This is where assuming the best and reminding yourself of their higher nature will help. Even if you're having trouble feeling genuine empathy, you can still soften any difficult feelings by reminding yourself that, well, they're only human. You don't have to like them or agree with them to acknowledge that they still can suffer, and that's reason enough not to want to be unkind to them!

Perhaps you're still irritated with your family member, but you feel more forgiving about the argument because you realize that they've had a tough life—tougher than yours in many ways—and that they're doing the best they can.

<u>Step 3</u>: The final step is compassionate empathy. Better than wallowing in someone else's emotions is to thoughtfully acknowledge them while improving the situation for everyone. This is where you make a suggestion to your family member so you can avoid the same kind of misunderstanding in the future. You might commit to making a kind and conciliatory gesture in a way you know they'll appreciate simply to mend the relationship and show goodwill. Maybe you calmly suggest that you both take a little time away from one another to cool off.

"Empathy in action" is where empathy really starts to impact our relationships. Trying to support the wellbeing of other people will help them, strengthen your relationship, and make you feel good, too! If people feel they are being heard and supported, they're far more likely to hear you and acknowledge *your* needs. It's a win-win.

If a close friend reveals that they have difficulty with agoraphobia, empathize with the fact, try to imagine what it must be like for them, and next time offer to meet them at their home instead of somewhere noisy and busy. If you get into an argument with an employee who isn't pulling their weight, first try to understand *why* they're behaving as they are. If you discover they're missing deadlines because of childcare issues, see what can be done to make their work schedule more flexible, or organize more work-from-home hours. If a partner feels insecure but you don't quite understand since you are self-assured, you could simply ask them what they need from you to feel more confident in themselves. The mere fact of you showing curiosity and respect for their perspective may be all the action that's needed!

Stay Curious

Okay, so we already know that successful communication means dropping the idea that other people are adversaries, enemies, or competitors. When we have empathy for them, we become curious about who they are and what their life is like. Curiosity is an unselfish orientation by nature—we turn our attention away from ourselves for a moment and place it on someone or something else. It's also a position that doesn't require ego or stubborn assumptions. Because if we're approaching someone in curiosity, we are saying *I don't know . . . but I'm interested in finding out.*

That means we're less likely to lead with our own assumptions, agendas, or theories about what people "should" be doing. We're less likely to barge ahead with our own perspective or trample over the other person's. Curiosity is a hopeful, creative mindset—it means we open our minds and prick our ears to new possibilities we haven't thought of yet, or imagine that things could turn out in novel, unexpected ways. Being curious is the state of mind where we confidently expect to learn something!

Be honest—when was the last time you experienced and expressed genuine interest in how someone else thought or felt?

Probably, you're more familiar with trying to make your viewpoint heard or waiting for the other person to speak so you can respond. But communication is the exchange of information. We're not merely swapping data we already know, we are trying to reach out into another person's world and learn something we *don't* know: Who are they? What are they about? What's going on with them?

If we already knew this (or *thought* we did), then there would be no point in communication.

You can practice being a more curious conversation partner immediately. The next time you're in discussion with anyone about anything, imagine emptying your head completely. See the situation at hand as new and fresh to you. Picture yourself as a scientist (or an alien! Perhaps an alien scientist?) trying to get to the heart of things.

The best way to do this is to ask questions. Lots of questions:

"Tell me more about . . ."
"What do you mean when you say . . .?"
"So, what do you make of this situation?"
"What are you trying to achieve here? Why?"
"I'm wondering about . . ."
"What made you make that decision?"
"What happened before this?"
"What do you think/feel about this particular fact?"
"What do you see as the main problem here?"
"What's your opinion on . . .?"

You can go a long way by saying things like, "I'm curious about . . ." or, "Help me understand." You'll simultaneously flatter people while making them feel heard and as though their opinion is valued. Remember the difference between observation and evaluation? It's crucial to keep value judgments out of the picture when you're asking questions. (In other words, don't ask things like, "Why on earth did you think that was a good idea?")

Often, we get so carried away in our perspective that, to be truthful, we simply don't care about what someone else thinks or feels. We're not interested in their take on things, and if we're honest, we don't especially value their ideas. But don't worry—being curious doesn't mean you condone actions you don't like, or that you rate a disagreeable opinion above your own. All you're doing is perceiving and becoming aware. That's the magic of curiosity—you're just asking questions. That's all.

Imagine you're working with someone you *really* don't get on with. Truth be told, you don't give half a damn about what they think, what they want, or why they do the (annoying) things they do. You just plain dislike them. And that's fine! But can you still be curious?

Staying curious keeps you open-minded and primes you to keep on the lookout for new solutions. It gives you insight into others, which at the very least gives you an edge in dealing with them. For example, you learn a little more about your colleague and realize that even though they're a pain in the rear to people in the office, they're an animal lover and have several pets they adore.

Great! You now have something to talk about with them that is low-stakes and likely to defuse or at least stall any conflict. You know what they value and can find more harmony and cooperation by simply appealing to this side. This could be nothing more complicated than strategically sharing details about your pet dog or asking their opinion on a dog-related topic. You do this not because you agree with them or like them, but because you want to get them alongside you and reduce potential friction in the workplace.

Curiosity helps you find that "third story" or that neutral, objective fact that grounds the interaction and stops it from veering off into tricky territory. It tells the other person that you're not interacting with an agenda or a preconceived notion about them. It communicates that you're aware of them as complex, nuanced people with views potentially different from yours (self-differentiation again!), and it also sends a strong message that you're comfortable and content enough in yourself to occasionally let the conversation dwell on someone else for a change.

One brilliant, practical way to use curiosity to diffuse tension or misunderstanding is to "play dumb." Don't make any assumptions but get people to spell things out to you loud and clear. Your assumptions are where the biases and expectations live. To combat these biases, ask what seems an obvious question or one you think you already know the answer to—you may be very, very surprised.

Ask them the same question in different ways to get different perspectives on the issue. Ask open-ended questions rather than yes/no questions. Don't put words into people's mouths—let them describe things in their terms. Paraphrase, often. For example, "You say that you felt this presentation was inappropriate. I was wondering what you meant by inappropriate, and you explained that you felt it might make some team members uncomfortable. Have I got that right?" This not only signals your respectful interest and curiosity, but it also shows people you genuinely care about getting the details right, and that you're not just pretending to be concerned.

And here we arrive at the most important part: true listening. When you ask a question, your role is not to interpret what you're told. It's not to figure out your rebuttal. It's not to decide if you agree or zone out while thinking about something else.

It's to listen. That's all!

Humility: The Rarest Virtue

And that takes us neatly to another real-world skill that will improve all your relationships: knowing when you're wrong and owning up to it.

If you see conversations as battles and your conversation partner as an opponent, then any hint that you're in the wrong will likely cause a defensive reaction in you. You might even assume that the other person pointing out your error is *attacking* you and respond in kind. If the goal of conversations is to bolster your ego, then making a mistake will feel like vulnerability, and it will seem like the conversation is now a failure.

However, if you see your goal as connecting meaningfully and compassionately with others, then you'll view any mistakes—your own or others'—as obstacles to connection that can be dealt with honestly and directly. Being mistaken doesn't mean you lose a point, and spotting flaws in the other person doesn't mean you gain one.

Like curiosity and compassion, humility is also a characteristic that people think is weak but is powerful. One of the best things you can do in relationships is learning to quickly accept when you're in the wrong and take responsibility for apologizing. Being wrong or called out can feel humiliating, enraging, or shameful for so many people. But it isn't! Making mistakes is the most boringly normal thing that humans do. How you *respond* to your own mess-ups is what makes the difference, however.

If this thing is difficult for you, start small by learning to say "I don't know" in conversations. Practice accepting and acknowledging small mistakes you've made. "Oops! I said Friday, but I meant Thursday."

These little concessions will make it easier to own up to the big mistakes and apologize more seriously. Psychology researchers Roy Lewicki, Beth Polin, and Robert Lount Jr. conducted two studies that suggested that an effective apology needed six key features:

Expressing regret and remorse ("I am so, so sorry for what I did, and I wish I could go back in time and change everything.")

Explaining what happened and why ("I was late that morning and rushing, and because I was on my phone, I didn't see your dog and ran over them in the driveway.")

Full acknowledgement of personal responsibility ("This was entirely my fault.")

Feeling repentant ("I have had a long hard think about what happened, and I am one hundred percent committed to never letting this kind of thing happen again. I have promised myself I won't even touch my phone in the car ever again.")

An offer to repair or make things right ("I will, of course, pay all the related vet expenses, or even the cost of another dog if that is something you'd consider.")

A request for forgiveness ("I know I can never bring your dog back, but I hope that in time you can forgive me. I never meant to hurt you or Lucky.")

One other factor is that the sooner you can demonstrate these elements, the better— and the more you've messed up, the sooner and more thoroughly you'd better tick each box. The most important is to accept full responsibility for what you've done. Nothing is more inflammatory than a faux apology where the person just blames someone or something else or makes lame excuses. The least important aspect is asking for forgiveness—it's best to do this only after you've done all the others, or else you're asking someone you've wronged to give *you* something, which is not exactly a good look.

But all this takes . . . you guessed it, humility. You need to swallow your pride and tell your ego to sit down. You don't need to beat yourself up or cover yourself in shame, though. This may come across badly. It's more effective to own up to what you did, rather than what you are. Don't get dramatic and say, "I'm an idiot," but say, "I did a stupid thing; it was a mistake." Dwelling on your own melodrama or how sad *you* are to have made the mistake is unlikely to work. Trying to make other people feel bad for you when you're to blame will also come across as manipulative, even if you genuinely are cut up by it all.

Be careful in your explanation not to squeeze in any excuses or minimize the problem. Have empathy and see the situation from their viewpoint. If the tables were turned, what would you most want them to say to you? Don't be passive or make it seem like things just happened ("I'm sorry you got your feelings hurt . . ."). Just rip the Band-Aid off and own up to your actions. Be plain and upfront.

Finally, once you've apologized, let it go. You cannot control how people take your apology, and they may not accept it at all.

That's their prerogative. Whatever you do, don't nag them for forgiveness or act entitled to be absolved just because you apologized. They will feel how they feel—*your* only job is to get clear in yourself and communicate your apology as best you can. Getting angry or disappointed with people because your apology didn't get the reaction you wanted is simply selfish. If you get a cool response to a heartfelt apology, just say, "I understand." No need to keep apologizing. The ball is now in their court.

The Patience to Let Others Be

Being a skillful communicator takes clear boundaries, empathy, curiosity, and a good dose of genuine humility for when you miss the mark. One final characteristic to master is patience. Sure, patience sounds like something boring and old-fashioned that only nuns are required to develop, but most of us could stand to be a lot more patient.

The world is set up to stimulate and sate a never-ending conveyor belt of desires, and given the nature of advertising, the media, and the internet, most of us are consistently trained to expect and seek instant gratification. It goes beyond the fact that we simply don't like waiting for what we want. Rather, it's about having the humility and broadened perspective to understand that you cannot demand everything moves at the pace *you* want it to move.

Some people are terrible listeners not because they don't care about other people's lives but because they have something akin to conversational ADHD. They lack patience and maturity and want to cut to the chase. Maybe they're impatient for the other person to stop speaking, so they can start. Or maybe they've convinced themselves they know what will be said and are just impatiently waiting for the conversation to finish. (Have you ever been on the receiving end of such impatience? It can be profoundly invalidating!)

Listening well means putting your own needs and perspectives on the back burner. Yes, really. It sounds boring, but this is a form of discipline that needs to be learned and practiced. There will simply be times when you are not the center of attention in any social situation, and where your wants, needs, and perspective are not the focus. More than that, there will just be times when you have to willfully put aside your own ideas about where the conversation should let the other person lead.

If you often feel impatient and irritable with people, ask yourself why. You might find your head filling with loads of "should" statements and prescriptive ideas about how you believe people should be. But dwell on what you're irritated about, and you'll see that it's not reasonable: you may be annoyed, essentially, *that other people are not like you*. They talk about topics you see as irrelevant, in ways you find strange or outright wrong, or at a pace you may think is too fast or slow.

But when you think about it, is that really a problem? Isn't this expectation a little like wanting everyone you meet to be a replica of yourself?

This point is subtle but goes deep, and it's a skill that many would argue is vanishing in the modern world. When you converse with someone, do you *make room* for them? Are you genuinely giving them space to speak, express themselves, and **be** as they are, without your judgment or interpretation or resistance?

Think of it in terms of attention. Imagine that attention is a valuable resource that everyone wants—we all yearn to be seen, acknowledged, and maybe even praised and appreciated for who we are. This is the main drive in many people's relationships! But if we approach every conversation as nothing more than an arena where we can extract this value from others, we are becoming precisely the person we don't want to encounter ourselves. In other words, we become self-absorbed and unable to listen.

This sets up a cycle. People are desperate for attention, but this need makes them so self-focused that they cannot give attention to others. What happens is that a conversation turns into a subtle competition for who can get the most airtime. Someone might dominate a conversation, interrupt others, and listen very little, then leave the conversation and, without a hint of irony, say, "Nobody ever pays me any attention."

The only way out is to be patient, be generous, and make space for other people. Not in the transactional sense ("if I listen to your boring nonsense for long enough, then you have to listen to mine"), but because making others feel heard and appreciated is just as enjoyable as feeling that appreciation ourselves.

Be kind to others. Some people you talk to will have been invalidated their entire lives and have never been seen or heard. But when both parties in a conversation are confident enough in themselves not to squabble for airtime, they can both relax and simply be with one another. Enjoying the limelight is then a lovely gift they take turns handing over to one another. There's always enough to go around.

At first, listening takes patience and forbearance. But if you practice, you'll soon realize that making others feel good, listening to them, making space for them and genuinely showing interest in them is not the awful punishment you first thought! You can derive a certain relaxed pleasure from stepping back and letting other people shine. Slow down. Make them feel seen and validated. Don't be in a hurry to speak or share every opinion or idea that pops into your head. You need not respond to everything or speak up whenever you disagree.

If someone doesn't return the favor and hogs attention forever? Well, that's what boundaries are for. Give people the benefit of the doubt but simply walk away if you consistently have to fight to be heard.

Here's a very practical way to bring more patience into your conversations: *every time you feel tempted to jump in and share your own opinion or anecdote, pause and ask a question instead.* Hit that tennis ball immediately back over the net instead of hogging it. You may discover that you feel closer and more connected to the other person, that you win their trust and liking, that you learn more about them, and that they're more interested in you—without you having to barge ahead in the conversation. This is ultimately worth much more than being the one that talks the most!

Takeaways:

- Better communication skills stem from a healthy mindset and a good attitude toward relationships in general.
- We can practice and communicate self-differentiation by knowing and taking responsibility for communicating our own needs. Then we can establish boundaries and gently but firmly assert them. Boundaries are not rules for others' behavior, but for ours.
- Empathy is the ability to understand and feel into someone else's experience and take action to help them. There are three types—cognitive, emotional, and compassionate.
- First, gain cognitive empathy by switching perspectives, listening, asking questions, and seeking to understand. Additionally, find emotional empathy by addressing their higher natures and assuming the best of them, or find common ground. Finally, offer

compassionate empathy by enhancing their wellbeing.

- We stay open-minded and humble with curiosity and approach others in a spirit of opportunity, respect, and the desire to learn. Express genuine interest in someone by asking open-ended questions and listening to the answers. Don't assume, let people speak, and check your comprehension by paraphrasing.

- Humility is the virtue that will allow you to quickly and sincerely own up to mistakes. This takes courage and maturity. Make sure any apologies show remorse, repentance, and full responsibility, and explain what went wrong, what you will do to fix it, and a request for forgiveness. Accept any response to your apology with grace.

- Practice conversational patience, listen to others, and give them the space to be as they are. Cut out the ego!

- You can validate others by asking questions every time you're tempted to jump in and hog attention. Relax, slow down, and have the self-discipline and compassion to let the conversation unfolds as it will, rather than as you think it should.

Chapter 3: What to Say and How to Say It

Even if you have the right mindset and the best of intentions, it will count for little if you're unable to effectively communicate your message. Communication is a skill. Though it may come naturally to some, it's an ability we have to consciously develop for most of us.

In this chapter, we'll be using the Imago framework to discuss healthier, more satisfying conversations—and look at what to say, when to say it, and most important, how to say it. This model was developed by Dr. Helen Hunt and her husband, Dr. Harville Hendrix, and has become a respected staple in marriage and family counseling the world over.

Understanding—and Removing—Emotional Barriers

We've considered at length the obstacles to our being empathetic, understanding and able to listen. Assuming the worst in others, being combative, and being poorly differentiated get in the way, as does a lack of empathy, curiosity, patience, humility, and boundaries.

All these obstacles to connection share an emotional root, however. The barriers to effective communication can be behavioral, cognitive, societal or even spiritual, but they all start as emotional barriers put up to keep us safe. If we want to connect with people, we must bring down those walls. Bringing down emotional barriers to connection is the main goal of communication.

One fundamental assumption of the Imago model is that we are not the only people in the world, our "reality" isn't the only one, and it's no more valid than anyone else's. While you may cognitively agree this is the case, it's another thing to feel it and practice it in the moment, when emotions are running high. If we find any obstacle to the complete acceptance of another person's equally valid reality, then we need to find a path back to that accepting mindset. Understanding, empathy, and cooperation happen once both parties are in complete acceptance.

Communication always entails a Sender, a Receiver, and the message itself. In Imago, there are three things that *a Receiver* has to do as the Sender is sending their message:

1. Mirroring
2. Validation
3. Empathy

These are not dissimilar from the stages of empathy described earlier. In the **mirroring** stage, you merely copy or mimic what the other person presents to show comprehension and listening. If they pause, you pause. You match and reflect their tone, and you say things like, "Okay, so it sounds to me like you're saying you're not angry it's broken, but angry that they didn't apologize?" or "Can you tell me more about why you feel so confused right now?" We stay neutral and non-judgmental.

We move to **validation** once we've completely heard the other person speak. Validation is simple: we tell the other person that what they've said makes sense, they have a right to feel that way, and their experience is valid. This doesn't mean you agree, however. It just means you can see, from their perspective, what they see. Validate content and their emotional interpretation (for example, "I can totally see how me not getting you a gift hurt your feelings and made you question our friendship. I wouldn't mind if someone didn't get me a gift, but I can see things from your point of view, and it makes sense that *you* feel that way").

If you don't understand, return to step 1 and clarify by asking more questions.
"Oh, I think I've misunderstood. You said you wanted an apology, but you also said earlier that you wouldn't accept one if it were given. Can you help me understand?"

The **empathy** step is where you try to put yourself in their shoes and feel what they're feeling. You might decide to add in an extra interpretation ("Do you think you're feeling lonely right now?"), but it's often best to simply reflect their feelings. Use feeling words but don't get too hung up on any particular label ("I can imagine you're feeling scared right now").

Here, you might like to pay attention to differentiate between feelings and thoughts and between fact and feeling. Just remember not to analyze or diagnose people—you're not trying to discover what you think about their viewpoint but what their viewpoint really is.

It's okay to help people pinpoint how they feel or guess at their emotions, but this can veer into invalidating territory. It's a good idea to listen closely to the words, terms, and metaphors they're using and reflect on them. If the person keeps describing a feeling as "worry," there's no use in introducing the term "anxiety"—even if you think this might be a better term. Remember, you're never trying to discover who or what is "right"— you're seeking to understand, connect, and bring down emotional barriers.

This process takes as long as it takes—it finishes when the Sender has adequately conveyed their message, and the Receiver has taken it all in. As a Receiver, your job is to give complete attention. Listen without interruption, interpretation, and judgment. There will be time to speak your piece later, but first, just seek to hear and understand. The Sender is in complete charge of where the conversation is going and what they're saying, **not you**. Keep your own agenda separate and only ask questions to clarify. In other words, when you are a Receiver, do just that—don't go into Sending mode yourself. Speak only when there is a long pause or the Sender signals they're done and want you to speak. You might like to end with something like, "Did I get that right?" or, "Is there anything more you need me to know?" to double-check that the Sender is finished.

Once that's done, you switch places, and it's the Receiver's turn to become the Sender. The Sender has an equally important role in the dialogue. Their job is to stay calm and clear and avoid getting carried away in reactivity. One tip: don't just launch into a dialogue without warning. Make an "appointment," i.e., ask if it's a good time to talk and schedule the conversation for when you both can give it your undivided attention. Ask rather than request. State your intention upfront and let them know what your message is and how you intend to send it. For example, "I want to have a discussion about your performance at work and the incident on Friday. I want this to be a respectful, win-win dialogue. When do you think would be a good time to chat?"

Now, wait. Give the other person time to receive, process, and respond. You, too, can practice mirroring and matching your tone and body language to theirs to demonstrate your commitment to harmony and cooperation. It's important to stay focused. If you're talking about work performance, then talk about that only and don't bring up unrelated grievances, side topics, or bygones that are irrelevant. One subject per conversation!

However, what's most important is to use the all-powerful "I" statements. Remembering the difference between evaluation and observation, and remember the need to stay self-differentiated and own your portion. Stick to describing *your* thoughts, feelings, and desires. Don't blame or tell other people what they feel or mean.

To talk about them, frame it carefully: "When you treat clients badly, **I feel** like I'm put in a difficult spot when I have to explain your behavior." This differs from saying, "You put me in a difficult spot." Don't inadvertently feed people a story about what should be or present your feelings as facts (e.g., "You don't care about this job and you don't respect me. That's your problem!"). "I feel unloved" is a world away from "you don't love me!" Simply stick to *your* experience and perceptions and remain non-accusatory and nonjudgmental.

If feelings are running high, it's difficult to do this without triggering defensiveness. That's why you need to plan ahead, go slow, and choose your words wisely. When you've said what you need to say, thank the Receiver for listening, to reinforce cooperative behaviors, and summarize your position before handing things over to them. Don't be afraid to politely but firmly assert yourself if they're trying to send instead of receive. "I'm sorry, I'm not done speaking yet."

As you can see for the respective "rules" for Sender and Receiver, this process works best when both people are on the same page, and both are operating from the same set of baselines assumptions. It may sometimes be worth outlining this explicitly first and laying some ground rules for effective dialogue, especially if matters have deteriorated badly already. However, communication "takes two to tango." If either party is unable or unwilling to listen, take turns sending and receiving, and remain focused on the goal of connection, then communication is unlikely to work. Here, it's okay to pause and schedule a conversation for another time. Remember— you cannot control other people.

Be on guard for your own tendency to jump in and interrupt with your corrections, justifications, explanations, interpretations, or disputes. Consciously set them aside— and don't spend your Receiving time stewing over a rebuttal instead of listening to what they're saying! If you are sending a message and the Receiver is interrupting, stay calm and assert a boundary. Be compassionate and forgiving but stay focused. "It's my turn to speak now."

Active Listening Techniques

Many marriage counselors and workplace mediators have experienced: someone earnestly tells them that they want to become better communicators, yet they are useless at listening to others. Why? Because they believe that a good communicator is good at making people hear them, instead of someone good at hearing other people. Big difference!

If you approach any conversation with the unspoken goal of getting others to listen to you, you've only got half of the puzzle. The biggest impediment to people doing "active listening" is the mistaken idea that they are already doing it. Blame it on our general attention deficit society or on the fact that none of us are ever deliberately taught this skill, but active listening is hard. It takes effort.

Active listening means giving your full and total attention to the speaker and listening to absorb, comprehend, respond to, and remember what you've been told. It's not just receiving a message, but taking that message, processing it, and doing something with it. And this applies to all of the message, including the nonverbal parts (the meaning conveyed in the tone of voice, body language, etc.), the words, and the content hidden *behind* the words.

We've already established that the goal of the conversation is not to serve your ego, find the winner/victor or hog the limelight. It's to connect, establish trust, learn something, or encourage cooperative and harmonious relationships. For ease, we can break down the skill of active listening into six skills, although in reality, these all blend into one another:

Non-judgment
This means keeping interpretations and evaluations out of the picture. To listen, you

want to receive what the other person is transmitting—your input is not required. No arguing, criticizing, or convincing. Observe rather than evaluate. This is challenging if the message you're sending contains upsetting or triggering information, but it's up to you to try not to go on the defensive. Whatever your position, calmly keep it to yourself until it's your turn to speak. Then use I statements and stick to facts rather than value judgments.

Reflection
Show that you're receiving the message loud and clear and that you're on the same page. If they're talking slowly and quietly, mirror them by doing the same. If they're talking in formal, professional terms, acknowledge this and follow. You might like to gently reflect their posture, too. Repeat their own phrases and terms back to you to show that you're "speaking their language"—literally.

Don't assume understanding. Literally ask, "Have I got that right?" to check your comprehension or paraphrase without adding extra data to reiterate what they're sharing. If someone says, "But I keep asking, and nobody listens! That's why I'm angry!" you can say, "So you're saying that you've raised this issue before, and it was ignored in the past? This is not the first complaint, right?" This gets people to say "yes," which creates the feeling of you both being on the same page. That feeling of commonality and understanding is a powerful springboard to reconciliation. It's less important to actively add to what they're saying.

Attention

Pause after people speak to show you aren't trying to jump in and blurt your opinion on what they've shared, and practice compassionate, accepting body language ("open" gestures and warm tone of voice). Don't be that person who isn't paying attention because they're too busy thinking what they'll say when the other person shuts up! This habit instantly puts people on the defensive and signals disrespect—and it's more noticeable than you think. Make eye contact, and whatever you do, don't get distracted by phones, screens, or other people passing by. *Stay present.*

Clarification

It's not a problem to misunderstand the other person or be unclear about their position. It's only a problem when these misunderstandings are not clarified. Ask questions rather than assume, since this demonstrates a willingness to genuinely understand their position. Keep questions respectful and open-ended without putting words into people's mouths. "Wait for just a second, I don't think I follow you. Can you go back to the part about your cousin and explain again how he fits into the story?"

As long as you frame your curiosity and misunderstanding as respectful rather than bringing in judgment (i.e., "You're not making sense. What are you talking about?"), then the other person will feel heard and validated. Even if you understand, carefully fleshing out the details shows that you're not barging ahead with your theories and assumptions. Even if you feel you know everything already, it's good to reiterate. "Okay, so let me just get clear on the whole story from the beginning . . ."

Summarizing

Revisit the main themes of what's been communicated, again without letting judgment or evaluation enter. Here, you can use the "third story" technique or imagine a neutral observer simply laying out the objective facts. Summarizing helps you put shape to issues and stay focused on one idea at a time. It gives you a chance to convey your understanding and check with the other person that you are gradually finding a shared position on which you can agree.

"So, let's see now. Melanie feels that she was explicitly asked to play a more active parenting role with her stepson Johnny, but Johnny's mother says that Melanie is overstepping and that her contribution is not required. Johnny's father is staying out of things, but it seems like both women are unhappy about this, as they want him to 'pick a side.' It seems like they both feel hurt and unsupported in this disagreement. They both want an apology, but neither wants to give an apology to the other. Have I got that about right?"

Sharing

This is done only once the other person feels sufficiently listened to. Sharing your own thoughts, feelings, suggestions, and perceptions can help the conversation, but only if it creates harmony and understanding rather than invalidating the other person's message. Talk about a similar experience you've had, share a slightly vulnerable side of yourself, or offer a conciliatory gesture. But again, if you share your own view before understanding the other person's, it's unlikely to come across well. "Not many people know this, but last year my wife and I experienced a miscarriage too, so I can understand to some degree how you must be feeling right now."

In disagreements or conflicts, many of us focus on what is wrong or lacking in the other person, unconsciously if our approach is already perfect, and they're the ones that need to change. We imagine that improving our conversation skills comes down to convincing them to see our viewpoint, without ever realizing the irony in this, and that we have consistently dismissed *their* viewpoint.

We need simple humility and honesty to see how we are not the skillful listeners we like to think we are. Signs that your listening could use some work:

- You often think about what you'll say next rather than paying attention to what the person is saying
- You simply talk most in conversations
- You launch into advice or suggestions before the other person has finished explaining
- You feel irked and dismissive when someone doesn't accept your advice or interpretations, wondering why they don't agree with you
- You find people's stories boring and have a hard time concentrating, imagining you already know what they're going to say
- You argue with people about what they're feeling and tell them not to feel that way (note, this can even be done in a caring way: "You're scared? Oh, don't be silly, you have nothing to be scared of. That's ridiculous!")

If you see some of yourself in the above, don't worry—it's perfectly human! Good listening skills can feel awkward and uncomfortable at first . . . but that's where humility and patience come in!

Try to imagine that the conversation is purely an exercise in listening. Don't think about your response until it's your turn to speak. This means being okay with silence and slowing right down. When you take your time, you also realize that you don't have to share every thought or opinion, and you don't have to cover everything in one conversation. There's no rule against coming back to the conversation later!

Listening closely for details but also emotional content. If you catch yourself going into Sender mode when you should be receiving, you can always say, "Sorry, I got carried away there! Please continue." Make encouraging sounds ("Uh huh," "I see"), but don't go overboard acting the part of a Good Listener! Just be present. Getting out of your own head and dropping your ego is often a way to reduce anxiety in a difficult situation—and it's *less* work! Try it. It can be such a relief to drop all agendas for a moment and simply focus on the other person.

Watch Out for Conflict Triggering Language

"Can you help me understand?"
"I'm Listening."
"We're on the same team."

In any context, can you see how hearing the above statements dissolves conflict and tension? How it instantly conveys an intention of collaboration and resolution? There are also phrases, words, and terms with the opposite effect—they trigger and invite conflict.

Words are powerful. Intention matters, but sometimes we can inadvertently communicate blame, criticism, or anger in unconscious or unintentional ways. Swearing and name-calling are hurtful, but plenty of damage can be done with subtle shifts in body language or tone of voice. Remember that your main goal in healthy communication is to establish a connection and bring down emotional barriers. These barriers can be subtle!

Don't say, "What's wrong with you?"

It's pure judgment, and it frames the other person as a problem. Nothing is wrong with them! When you blame others this way, you set yourself up as a default neutral and the other person as the one needing to change. Do this, and you can guarantee a defensive response.

In fact, avoid "you" as much as possible, especially in delicate or emotional situations. "You did XYZ" or "you are being unfair" naturally trigger the other person to go into defense, and instantly the barriers come up. In a conflict situation, don't assign blame or be too quick to diagnose the situation according to your own biases and assumptions. "You're just like your mother . . ." "I bet you're loving all this drama!" You are in the situation together, and nobody is "the problem."

Instead, say, "Help me understand what's happening here."

Maybe they're late again, or they've lied. You genuinely cannot make sense of their behavior, and you're frustrated. But don't lash out. Try to have compassionate understanding and ask questions to see why they're behaving as they are. "You keep doing that even though I've asked you not to. Why is that happening? I don't want to make you feel bad, but it's frustrating, and it doesn't make sense to me. Help me understand what's happening here." This way, you truthfully express your frustration without making the other person wrong.

Don't say, "I'm sorry if you took it that way."

What a way to dodge accountability! This is a statement almost guaranteed to infuriate people, along with related statements such as "I'm sorry you got hurt" or "I'm sorry you misunderstood what I was saying." If you say this, be honest; chances are there is a covert desire to communicate the opposite of "sorry." Don't be passive aggressive!

If you squeeze in that "if," you're invalidating the other person and making their grievances seem trivial, doubtful, or even hypothetical. If someone says, "I'm hurt," and you say, "I'm sorry if you feel hurt," you have effectively negated their statement. They *do* feel hurt; there's no "if" to it!

Phrases like this absolve you of responsibility and throw the blame back in the other person's face . . . and they'll likely only feel angrier. For similar reasons, avoid saying, "I'm sorry, but . . ." Think of *but* as a word that cancels out everything that came before it. Instead, commit to stopping the sentence before the *but*. "I'm sorry."

Instead, say, "I'm sorry I hurt you/did that."

Apologize without caveats, conditions, or qualifications. As we've seen, owning up fully to your responsibility is the best way to apologize. A weaselly half-apology that puts underhanded blame on the other person is worse than no apology.

Don't say, "Why are you so upset by this?"

Remember that people's realities are as valid as yours. They feel what they feel, and it's never up to you to sit in judgment of those feelings or evaluate whether you think they should be allowed to have them. Never, ever tell people they are "overreacting." This is often said as an underhanded attack to invalidate and diminish the other person—passively. Don't do it! Especially don't do it if the other person is upset because of something you've done.

Try not to be that person who takes secret pleasure in rattling or upsetting others while you sit calm and composed, feigning shock at their strong, out-of-control emotions. This is a power play, plain and simple. Even if they can't articulate why, people can sense this and will respond defensively.

Don't push people and then claim you were "only joking." Don't rile people up only to act like their valid anger is the problem and not your provocation. Finally, avoid the damaging habit of framing your perspective as objective fact while labeling the other person's perspective as "irrational." Saying things like "I'm just being logical here" or "calm down" is emotional warfare and will get a predictable result—you'll inflame the situation, lose trust, and come across as a jerk.

Instead, say, "I understand why you feel that way."

When you are a properly differentiated person, you allow other people to have the emotions they have. You never even consider that it's in your scope to permit anyone to feel what they feel. You're secure enough in yourself and your feelings not to jump in and judge, interpret, or analyze. You realize that it's simply not your job to decide whether or not you agree with them, or whether they are right. The point is only to hear and witness.

Don't say, "You always do this, I always do that . . ."

"Always" and "never" are red flags for all-or-nothing, black-and-white thinking, and they signal a break down in nuanced understanding and a descent into oversimplification. These terms act as emotional barriers because they're just not true. If person A says, "You never clean the kitchen!" then what will person B say? "That's not true! I cleaned it that weekend in May 1998." Where does that leave everyone?

Using absolute terms is a way of painting the situation or the other person in a broad brush, either to feel superior and righteous or to simplify a complex situation.

Instead, say, "What I need is . . ."

Instead of dumping negative feelings on the other person (and inviting a retaliation), clearly state what you need in that moment. "I feel like all the housework falls on me, and I'm exhausted. I feel so sad, like my time isn't important. What I need is for you to do your fair share of the chores." Extreme statements are like spears, and often they're hurled to hurt the other person rather than reach an understanding. If you're hurt, say so. Don't launch into blame or foregone conclusions. Remember that it's possible to feel hurt *without someone hurting you.*

Don't say, "Whatever."

In a healthy conversation, both parties take responsibility, and both show up as full participants. Saying, "I don't mind/care" or "you can choose" is a sneaky way of absolving yourself of responsibility while pretending to be accommodating. For bonus damage, say "I don't mind" when you *do* mind and then subtly punish the other person for not doing what you wanted!

Trying to duck out of the conversation is a hostile act and signals to the other person you want them to take on all the emotional labor, or that you will go along, but will drag your feet and make them regret expecting anything from you. This is no more sophisticated than a child throwing themselves on the floor and refusing to move when unhappy.

Not having an opinion, not deciding, and not pulling your weight puts the burden on the other person and indirectly communicates a dismissive attitude to maintaining that relationship. It's a recipe for resentment—on both sides.

Instead, say, "Give me a moment to think about this."

It's okay to feel unsure or undecided. But don't wriggle out of active, adult participation in your relationships. Ask for time to think things over or make your decision—but don't forfeit your responsibility or right to a decision. Commit to a position and then stick to it. Be honest if you're trying to avoid conflict or disagreement by being "easygoing." If so, you might need to speak up about your desires, or simply accept that there is sometimes disagreement. Look for compromises. Don't be afraid to put forward your own idea or suggestion.

Don't say, "Well, actually . . ."

By now, you should recognize this word for what it is: an attempt to make your reality and perspective the "right" one so you can correct and educate everyone else. Arrogant, right?

"I've paid the bill for us for the last four times, and I . . ."
"Actually, it was only the last three times."
"Uh . . . okay."

Using "actually" this way is a sign of viewing the conversation as a fact-finding mission, and a contest to establish the most correct (often, the most intelligent) person. Be prepared to encounter resistance and defensiveness. In the above exchange, the intended content is being ignored while the person fixates on largely irrelevant details. It's not a quiz show, and no points are being awarded.

Instead, listen for the emotional content and avoid "correcting" people on things that are not really in the realm of objective information. It's a bad idea to try to inform people what they think and feel, or assume that you're entitled to educate them about their position. This is especially egregious when the person you're talking to has an experience or perspective you can genuinely never understand, or if they have a legitimate grievance with you.

Instead. say, "I see things differently."

It's not about facts. Don't pounce with glee on people's small mistakes. As they say, would you rather be right or be happy? Sometimes, that's what it comes down to! If the fact doesn't matter, then just drop it.

Don't say, "Well, you're entitled to your opinion."

Ah, how kind and generous of you to grant someone permission to have their own opinion! As king of the universe, that's awfully nice of you. Jokes aside, this and related phrases ("You do you!" or, "Well, if *that's* what you want to believe . . .") are solid gold invalidation. You won't come across as tolerant—quite the opposite.

Instead, say nothing!

You don't need to *tell* someone you respect their opinion. Show them. The best way to show them is to . . . listen.

Test Your Assumptions

You may try hard to acknowledge that the other person has an equally valid reality, and do your best to see into that reality and understand it. Yet things get murky when we approach conversations with untested assumptions—especially assumptions we don't even know we have.

We can be well-intentioned and genuinely mean to understand and connect with someone, but in doing so, rely on our interpretations and mental models instead of listening and perceiving what is right in front of us. When we make assumptions and theories about other people's intentions and emotions, we are in dangerous territory and may not realize it. It's easy to fill in the blanks, to guess at what other people mean, or to assume that their understanding of a concept is identical to ours.

We may not even realize that we've jumped to conclusions until we're rudely confronted with a misunderstanding. It takes humility, patience and an open mind to realize that other people inhabit different worlds, with ways of thinking and being that can be alien to us. It's not only arrogance or a desire to control that makes us assume we know others better than we do—we may make this mistake simply in our eagerness to understand. We can only interpret others according to our own values and past experiences, but this can sometimes mean we miss the mark.

One example of failing to appreciate another person's reality is the tendency to **psychologize**. This is tricky because it's hard to spot; emotionally intelligent and self-aware people may not realize that they are forcing certain explanations, analyses, or ideas onto others.

Consider Person A, who believes themselves to be a good listener and a "people person" and has a psychology background and some experience in the helping professions. They encounter Person B, who is less emotionally intelligent, less articulate with expressing their feelings, and less familiar with the popular psychological jargon of the day. In a disagreement, Person A takes issue with

Person B's behavior and says something like this:

"Why won't you talk to me? You just bottle everything up. You're so *avoidant*. If you don't express yourself, you'll just blow up one day when it's too much. You've always been like this. It comes from your upbringing—I don't know, maybe you need to think about why you're so afraid of opening up. Is it that you don't trust me? Why?"

From Person A's viewpoint, they are being honest and communicative, they are asking questions, they are showing compassionate concern, and they are doing all the right things . . . but can you see the problem? Though they don't mean to, Person A has made a whole world of assumptions about Person B's character, intentions, thoughts, and feelings. They have not only barged in with an intrusive analysis of Person B's behavior, but they have also used this to push ahead with advice and suggestions on how to fix themselves.

Person A may be surprised to find that Person B does not appreciate or respond well to being told so directly who they are and what their lives mean. Is it really for Person A to make a definitive pronouncement on Person B's experience in this way? Isn't that Person B's job? In making models and theories about why people behave as they do, we miss the opportunity to ask them and listen to their answers. We also pathologize them—a label like "avoidant" can do as much damage as a more obvious insult!

Even if—and especially if—we feel we are trying to understand people, we need to be careful that we're not overstepping and psychologizing them, picking them apart, explaining their experience to them, or assuming we may describe them or their narratives. We need to get out the way so the other person can speak for themselves and put forward their own reality, on their own terms.

Person B: "Uh, I *do* talk and share my feelings. But you don't listen. So now I just shut up!"

Another way this dynamic can play out is when we allow untested assumptions to lead us to unflattering conclusions about other people.

"You always turn down alcohol when I offer it to you, and now you want to leave the party early. Why are you being so antisocial?"

"You're spending Christmas with her and not me. How could you do that to me? Why would you want to hurt me like that?"

"It's our third date tonight, and you know what *that* means."

"I gave him some constructive feedback last week, so that's obviously why he's being so cold with me now."

"I teased her in front of all her friends, and she yelled at me. She's probably just embarrassed!"

In the above examples, assumptions have been made, and there's a good chance they're incorrect. The person turns down alcohol because they're a recovering alcoholic, not because they're antisocial. She yelled at you because she was angry that you had made fun of her in front of her friends, not because she was embarrassed. And so on.

When you're in dialogue, you need to assume nothing as far as possible. Especially don't assume what other people are feeling, what they're thinking, why they behave as they do, what they want, their values, what they think of you, or how they understand the world. Though some people like to imagine they are, nobody is psychic—the *only* way to know about a person's reality is to ask them. And the only way to see whether your assumptions are correct is to test them.

Question yourself.
Question others.

Don't just go with your first instinct. The most harmful assumptions are those stubborn ones you don't even notice yourself holding. Get into the habit of asking yourself, "What's the evidence?" Stop and look closely if you catch yourself going into explanations, interpretations, judgments, and analyses about others. What do you one hundred percent know? And what have you just . . . made up?

As we've seen, we learn about people's experiences by communicating with them, not by going deeper into our heads. Paraphrase, ask clarifying questions, and stay open-minded.

Listening and Nonviolent Communication

Let's end this chapter by reinforcing the principles we've hinted at throughout and looking at a few final tips and hints. These principles are part of communication expert Marshall Rosenberg's "non-violent communication" framework:

Listening is a path into another person's world.

Force invites resistance. But curiosity and respect invite cooperation and trust. Simple as that! Always begin by laying a foundation: a solid understanding of where the other person is coming from. Only then can effective negotiations, discussions, and conflict resolutions take place.

Show empathy by reflecting that worldview back.

When we listen, we understand a person's perspective. When we bounce that perspective back to them, we *show* them we understand. Paraphrase, summarize, and mirror body language, voice, and word choice. Validate the other person by confirming that you see that their interpretation makes sense, and that their perspective is valid. Generously use phrases like "that's right" and "yes, of course! I understand."

Gain clarity and focus by labeling feelings.

As you paraphrase and summarize, put words to feelings, demonstrating your empathy and desire to understand. "It seems like . . ." or "I wonder if . . .?" show a willingness to enter the other person's world and register their emotional reality. In conflict, everyone can lose their sense of self-differentiation, but this can be regained when we slow down, correctly label thoughts and feelings for what they are, identify fact and opinion, and correctly attribute emotions and thoughts to the people they belong to.

Lead any negotiation or conflict-resolution attempt by acknowledging fault and addressing the worst misgivings first.
Humbly accept, from the very beginning, your responsibility and culpability. Anticipate and prepare your response to people's objections and accusations, then proactively face them head on. It may be a little nerve-wracking, but it fosters trust, deeper intimacy, and a sense of honesty. It signals to the other party you are open to compromises, ready to accept your portion of blame, and embarking with as little ego as possible.

The biggest killer of effective communication is judgment.
Observe, don't evaluate. If your goal is connection, understanding and harmony, then blame, shame, and ego have to go. Work as hard as you can to stay aware of the tendency to judge, morally condemn, analyze, interpret, or classify others as good or bad. "You're mean" is an evaluation,

whereas "you often raise your voice to waiters" is an observation. Flex your own sense of self-differentiation by taking responsibility for yourself and avoiding blaming others or collapsing into shame.

When you catch yourself (or someone else!) being judgmental, remind yourself of the fact that judgment is just a poor method of getting needs met. Forget the judgment and look at the need. Then address that need directly. Making others feel bad inferior may feel good temporarily, but it damages your connection and will only invite defensiveness.

"I" statements are your savior here. Also, watch out for expressions like, "You made me so angry." It's not true! Nobody can *make* you feel anything. "I feel angry" is more accurate and centers you back in your agency. In conflicts and arguments, it's tempting to blame other people or the world at large for our actions. A clue is when you say things like, "I don't want to, but I *have* to . . ." or "I probably shouldn't, but . . ." Instead, acknowledge that you have chosen to do what you've done. This way, you are empowered to change and improve. Claim your own self-responsibility and grant other people the right to theirs.

The four steps of non-violent communication

These are:

Observations
Feelings
Needs
Requests

In that order. Observe the neutral and objective situation in front of you without judgment or interpretation. Become aware of people's feelings in the matter. Explore your own needs and the needs of others (hint: if communication is an attempt to get needs met, then meeting everyone's needs is the fastest way to a successful conversation), and finally make respectful and reasonable requests of others, or meet theirs.

Let's look at each step in turn.

Step 1: Observations

Not evaluations or judgments. Imagine you're a neutral observer telling a third story. Your goal is to describe and understand—the rest is just opinion.

"I notice that you spend most evenings looking at your phone after dinner. During this time, you don't talk much to the family or me."

Step 2: Explore Feelings
Not "opinions." Watch out for the word "should"—having an opinion about how other people should behave is one thing, but it's not a feeling. Express what you feel about what you've observed, but avoid interpretations and assessments of what you observe, or laying blame. Simply stick to how you feel.

"When you pay attention to your phone like that, I feel really sad. I start to feel insecure in our marriage."

Be careful—"I feel you're being dismissive" or "I feel you should care more about family time" are not feelings; they're claims and opinions. "I feel like you don't care" is also tricky since it is attempting to read the other person's mind or guess their perspective. Watch out for feeling words that are thinly veiled accusations or interpretations: ignored, abused, manipulated, misunderstood, rejected, threatened, and so on.

Does your feeling word imply the other person's action? Choose a word that focuses exclusively on your inner feelings instead. For example, grateful, calm, happy, afraid, bored, embarrassed, jealous, overwhelmed, excited. These do not implicate any person. A good trick to get a handle on this is to structure your sentence: "I feel X" rather than "I feel *that* X," which is usually an opinion or judgment.

Step 3: communicate needs

What do your feelings say about your unmet needs? Clarify this for yourself. Underneath all feelings are unmet needs. Good feelings signal our needs are met; uncomfortable feelings signal they aren't. We all need safety, respect, autonomy, understanding, love, support, and so on. But we can communicate these natural needs directly without resorting to trying to control, blame, or manipulate others into meeting our needs indirectly. Understanding your needs requires self-awareness and honesty.

"I feel insecure because I need quality time, love, and attention."

This sentence expresses feelings without judgment and connects the feeling with unmet needs. Try using the format: "I feel X *because* I need Y." Stick to "I" statements and avoid using "you." For example, avoid "I feel bad because *you* keep ignoring me."

Exploring needs also means learning to hear other people's unmet needs. If you feel criticized, controlled, or attacked, it's a powerful skill to listen for the unmet needs behind it. There's no need to blame yourself or the other person. In this example, the husband could hear his wife's unmet needs for affection even if she communicates inelegantly and tells him, "You're rude, and you don't care about me!"

Be the bigger person and listen for feelings and unmet needs. "Are you saying I'm rude because you need to feel loved right now?" Tuning into needs this way always diffuses tension, anger, and reactivity and steers the conversation to what matters: getting everyone's needs met. Ask yourself in any encounter, *what are my feelings here? What are theirs? How are these feelings connected to our needs?*

Step 4: Requests
Only once all the other steps are complete, can you start making requests or appeals.
"Could you put away your phone after dinner and talk to the kids and me?"
It may also be your turn to hear and respond to requests. Requests aren't a guarantee of getting what you want—but if you communicate non-violently, the chances are always better.

Takeaways:

- In the Imago framework, we seek to remove emotional barriers to connection by communicating. The Sender and the Receiver take turns sharing their message.

- The Receiver listens by mirroring, validating, and communicating empathy as the Sender speaks. Then, they change places. The key is to be patient, not interrupt, and avoid trying to be the Sender when acting as the Receiver.
- Active listening techniques help us absorb, understand, remember, and respond to what we're told. This includes non-judgment, reflection, paying attention, seeking clarification, summarizing, and possibly sharing your own experience.
- It's important to avoid using language that triggers defensiveness. This includes things like "what's wrong with you?" "I'm sorry you feel that way," "whatever," "you're overreacting," "you're entitled to your opinion," or anything using absolute terms like "always" and "never." These are invalidating and inflammatory and will be met with resistance, emphasizing emotional barriers rather than dissolving them.
- Immersing yourself in someone else's equally valid reality is harder than it looks, and so we need to test our own

assumptions routinely. We need to ask people questions and challenge our own assumptions about what they think or feel or how we attribute their actions.

- Psychologizing people is a way we can believe we're listening compassionately, but actually, we're forcing our interpretation or worldview onto another person instead of genuinely listening to their experience.
- The four principles of Marshall Rosenberg's non-violent communication are: observations, feelings, needs, and requests, in that order.
- First, make neutral observations instead of judgmental evaluations. Next, seek to explore feelings and not opinions. Be careful about using "you" statements or attributing blame, and instead take responsibility for your own experience. Next, connect your feelings with any unmet needs with the format: "I feel X because I need Y." Finally, end with a respectful and reasonable request focused on your needs.

Chapter 4: How to Own Your Emotions

Let's return to a question we began this book with: what is communication, anyway? Really, what is the point?

People reach out to one another because, in the nonviolent communication framework, they're attempting to get their needs met. Whether that need is for validation, affection, respect, security, or attention, people communicate because they're trying to cope and survive in the world and establish control over their surroundings. Even a tiny baby knows how to do this—they will scream and cry to get others to satisfy their needs for care and attention.

Behind *every* attempt at communication is an expression of need:

Posting several selfies and updates on social media daily—"I need to feel important. I need validation."

Sending a nit-picky, micromanaging email to a colleague—"I need to feel in control of this process."

Making a hurtful remark to a friend celebrating an achievement—"I need to feel like I'm good enough, too."

Beneath even the less flattering needs that people have to feel superior, dominate, control, or possess, there is usually a simpler need to feel safe and loved. The person trying to blame you for something that's not your fault needs to make you the bad guy . . . but this comes from a deeper need to just feel better about themselves.

Relationship problems stem not from the fact that we have needs, or that other people may need us to address their needs, but from our imperfect communication of those needs. If we deeply crave reassurance and safety, for example, but in our fear, we lash out and push people away, our communication approach is not working. In this sense our communication is "bad"—but our need itself is never wrong.

Relationship issues and poor communication often feature a misunderstanding of what communication is *for*—we instead use it to control people, force them to behave in the way we think they should, pull them closer or keep them away, and elicit from them things we want. But we don't need to do this. It can be a complete revelation when you understand that **you are totally able to meet your own needs**.

Yes, sometimes you need others to help you or comply with requests, but this won't happen unless you understand your own needs, proactively communicate them and ask for the support you need. Self-knowledge, proper boundaries, and the ability to accurately convey your state of mind to others—these are things *you* are in charge of.

So, paradoxically, the path to connecting with others is through a deeper connection with yourself. The best way to live interdependently and cooperatively with others is to dig deep and find your inner autonomy and self-differentiation. This way, you navigate the changing flow of self and other, and of intimacy and distance, but without conflict or drama.

Here's a liberating idea: you possess everything you need to be a happy, well-balanced person who can form meaningful and satisfying relationships with others. Nobody needs to *give* this feeling to you from the outside. However, you will develop this power within yourself, and if you don't actively strive to remove obstacles and impediments, you are doomed to keep living with them.

In this chapter, we'll look at the four reasons people fail to "own their shit" (forgive the crudeness, but this phrase gets to the heart of the matter!). Instead of taking ownership of their strengths and weaknesses, of their agency, of their feelings and desires, they get entangled with others in confusing and unhealthy ways:

Obstacle 1: You have no idea what your stuff even is (and so can't own it).

Obstacle 2: You know what your stuff is, but because of low self-worth, passivity, a victim mentality, or an unconscious need to be rescued, you don't feel entitled to claim your feelings . . . or take responsibility for yourself.

Obstacle 3: You're confused about what is your stuff and what is others', i.e., you are poorly self-differentiated and need others to tell you what to think or feel. Or you go the other way and tell others what they think and feel.

Obstacle 4: You know what your stuff is but can't stop doing it—you're trapped in maladaptive habits stemming from childhood and seem to go round and round in the same loops and patterns.

Truthfully, these could be an issue for you! But have no fear, there are concrete, effective ways to get a handle on even the most stubborn obstacles to being the communicative, happy, and well-connected person you were always meant to be. In previous chapters, we looked at the communication process itself, but here we'll be diving into some potentially tender and difficult material all about who we are deep down.

You'll know that "relationship problems" are really "me problems" if VERB feelings dominate your life: acting like a **V**ictim, **A**cting entitled, awaiting **R**escue and **B**laming. If your relationships abound with feelings of neediness, passivity, and being "clingy," then this is also a clue. Do you constantly look to others to give you permission on what to feel . . . or whether to feel at all? Do you seek reassurance and feedback, or constantly check in to confirm your own feelings or opinions? Finally, do you have trouble with perfectionism and being overly critical of yourself? This might hint at a deeper problem: it's not in your relationships with others, but your relationship with yourself.

Getting off the Projection Carousel

Let's look at obstacle 1—not knowing yourself. Becoming good in relationships and a better communicator *is the same thing* as becoming a more self-aware, more evolved, and more self-actualized individual. Imagine that your relationships with others are a mirror held up to your relationship with yourself.

If you don't own your emotions, they're still there, and they still have all the same influence over you—you're just unaware of it! And what you're unaware of is outside your control. Psychotherapist Carl Jung said, "Until you make the unconscious conscious, it will control your life, and you will call it fate."

For example, you choose but believe someone else "made" you do it. You assume they are in control of your life, and get to work arguing with them, never realizing that your state of mind was never their responsibility.

One way to bring the unconscious out into the conscious (where you can *do* something about it) is to work with your shadow and commit to cutting down on projection. Carl Jung was the first to talk about the "shadow," i.e., the part of your psyche that you've disowned and disinherited, pushing it out of conscious awareness. The shadow contains things we are ashamed or fearful of and things we haven't yet processed. Healthy, mature people realize that they are a mix of both good and bad and can accept that they are flawed and have a dark side. But if there is a fact about ourselves we can't handle, it gets pushed out of awareness and into our shadow where we no longer see it.

Yet, it is still there and makes its presence known in dreams or when we project it onto others. A simple example is someone who has difficulty accepting their own sexual orientation, and from a sense of shame, cuts it off of their identity. This part of themselves goes into the dark and into the shadow. They then find themselves extremely judgmental and hostile toward gay people, heaping scorn that seems disproportionate. Why? Because to protect their ego, they have disowned their unacceptable desires and projected them out into the world onto someone else, where it's safe. Their homophobia in the outside world reflects the intolerance they feel for an aspect of themselves.

Effective communication and self-differentiation mean being willing to work on your own shadow and own up to what is yours. It would be useless to have endless heated "conversations" with those you have projected onto—they are not even really conversations but a rehearsal of our inner dialogue with our shadow. Listen to the above person arguing about homosexuality and imagine that they are not arguing with the other person but with a disowned part of themselves.

If your shadow is out of conscious awareness, though, how could you ever identify it?

It's tricky. But try to look for disproportionate, intense, and *automatic* responses to stimuli that feel almost irrational. Look for defensiveness and resistance in yourself—as though your unconscious mind is saying, "Don't look over here!" Commit to pausing and refusing to assume that the source of the defensiveness is in the external environment or another person. "Hang on . . . why am I getting so upset about this?"

For example, someone may feel guilty, assume that everyone is accusing them, and react angrily to every imagined slight. This is a clue that a nerve has been struck and that they are close to learning something that their mind would prefer to remain oblivious to (i.e., their uncomfortable feelings of guilt). Here, they have a choice:

1. continue to solve the problem by going into conflict with all the people they believe are accusing them
2. go within and explore where this feeling of being accused *really* comes from

The first approach will escalate and maintain conflict; the second will diffuse it.

Doing "shadow work" is a technique beyond the scope of this book but is a powerful way to take ownership of those most irrational, most stubborn biases, blind spots, and denials. For the time being, you can become curious about your shadow by simply noticing whenever you feel triggered and defensive.

At first, you may have to keep reminding yourself, "Is this my stuff? Or their stuff?" In time, you'll better recognize what role you're playing in any interaction, which will lead to deeper self-knowledge. Imagine the process as one of recalling and owning all the fractured, disinherited parts of your personality. We dissolve the shadow not by vanquishing it, but by shining the light of consciousness on it and accepting it as part of ourselves.

Doing so means you stop projecting this material onto others and that you become better at recognizing when others are projecting onto you. You can be like the person yelled at by a stranger in the street but can genuinely stay calm, shrug, and say, "I am not the cause of or the source of that person's anger. His reaction has nothing to do with me." You are not hooked into their drama; you pass by unaffected, knowing it is theirs.

Meet Your Own Needs

Let's look at obstacle 2—being unable to own your feelings because of a sense of passivity, worthlessness, victim mentality, or a deep need to be rescued. This attitude usually has deep roots in childhood, where we may have learned that everything we need or want is always outside of ourselves, and if we want to survive, be happy, or feel good, we need to somehow convince people who are better and more powerful than us to *give* us that feeling. Thus, we always feel weak, anxious, and at the mercy of others. We want to be taken care of, but simultaneously we may resent the passive role and never quite feel confident in ourselves or relationships. Hence, we constantly ask for reassurance. It's a recipe for low self-esteem.

At the very core of this mindset is the belief that other people can (or should!) solve your problems for you. The flip side is that you feel that all your problems result directly from other people, and so only they hold the key to fixing the issue and allowing you to be happy. Either way, you are wholly disempowered and lack autonomy.

You forfeit your own power in any situation and play at being more helpless than you are. There are advantages to this: you never have to face tough decisions yourself or get real about your own culpability because you can simply point to another person and say, "Well, what can I do?" You might feel morally vindicated and unconsciously relieved that you don't have to take any action to solve problems yourself. But there are big disadvantages, too: a creeping sense of low self-esteem and powerlessness is the price you pay.

Getting out of victim mentality is a challenging path, but it can be done—you may discover that the very thing you feared claiming (i.e., responsibility) was the thing you were missing and longing for in life. The more ownership and responsibility you take, the more empowered you feel, plus confident and self-assured. The truth is that we all *co-create* our relationships—relationships are never done *to* us. We are one hundred percent responsible for our portion of any relationship we create. How you respond to others is a choice you make and not a foregone conclusion you have no say in.

When you take responsibility for your life, you don't wait around for someone to victimize you, nor to rescue you from that victimization. You don't frame relationships as dramas where everyone's assigned the role of victim, perpetrator, or savior, but see them as voluntary engagements between equals.

How do you know if you have underlying issues with passivity or a victim mentality? Well, notice if you bristled a little or felt indignant reading the above description. Did you experience any immediate reaction, any resistance, or even any outright hostility? Maybe you thought something like, "Fine, but I really *am* a victim . . . have you met my ex?" If so, look closely at your resistance!

Undoing these core beliefs takes time, but you can do a lot by consciously meeting your own needs wherever possible. Get into the habit of turning within and relying on yourself to emotionally regulate, rather than defaulting to other people. As in nonviolent communication, ignore the surface-level details of any conflict or argument and instead ask, "What are my deepest needs here? What needs am I trying to meet right now?" You might notice how often your behavior is an indirect attempt to have people listen to you, to care, or to validate you.

Most important, try to meet those needs for yourself without trying to engage another person. If you notice yourself essentially begging someone to make you feel better, ask what you're missing, and commit to making yourself feel better. Do you need assurance? Think of things you can do for yourself that make you feel more confident. Whether you successfully meet your own needs is irrelevant—the power comes from flexing your autonomy muscle and reminding yourself that you always have the ability to choose.

If you identify and own your emotional needs, you become less likely to push these onto others. Keep returning to the following framework:

1. What do you feel right now? (*You*, not the other person)
2. What unmet need is creating this feeling?
3. What can you do to address this need immediately?

For example, you're having a tense and awkward conversation with a partner. They say, "Look, I don't want to talk about this now. I'm going out. We can have this conversation tomorrow, okay?" In that moment, you pause and go through the framework:

1. You're feeling abandoned, panicky, and rejected. There's a feeling of being unloved and unlovable.
2. This feeling signals an unmet need: the need to feel valued, cared for, safe, loved, and appreciated.
3. You give yourself this feeling. You disengage from the conversation, step aside to calm down for a moment, and then do some journaling or

affirmations ("I'm enough as I am. I'm safe.") Maybe you do things you know make you feel better, like chat with friends, take a long walk, play with pets, or make art.

Something special happens somewhere between steps 2 and 3: you realize that the other person is not your sole source of good feelings or the only way to meet your needs. You don't have to cling, argue, beg, or control. You can meet your needs yourself, or in some cases, get someone or something else to meet them. There is no problem and no need for conflict. "Okay, I understand. You need some time to cool off. Let's chat tomorrow after dinner. I'll head out for a walk."

Children rely on adults to address their needs. But adults are capable of meeting their own.

Do what you can to own and fulfill your own emotional needs, and drop blame, control, and manipulation. You could go on the defensive and get upset, force a breakup, or even threaten suicide to control the situation. This may work in the short term, but you will just play out the same dynamics repeatedly unless you are acting from your own autonomy. Every time you blame others, you give them the power to determine your experience, and rob yourself of the opportunity to determine your experience for yourself.

Have the Courage to be Yourself

Obstacle 3 is allowing—or requiring—other people to tell you how to think and feel. This is the person who cannot state their opinion without first checking to see what others' opinions are. It's when we rate other people's perspectives as more important, more real, or simply better than ours. We even allow others to decide what we like, think, and what our lives mean.

This can be tricky to spot in action because people *are* interconnected and mutually dependent to some degree. We all influence and affect one another, and healthy individuals know there is always some give and take in relationships. However, it's a problem when we literally feel like we don't know who we are, and other people's mindsets, beliefs, feelings, and perspectives dominate over ours. For example, a woman buys a new dress that she thinks looks amazing on her. She confidently shows it to her husband, who declares it hideous. She immediately takes on his judgment as her own without even realizing it. "Yeah, you're right, I don't know what I was thinking. It is kind of ugly."

Not confidently communicating our needs and desires can come from low self-esteem, but it's also a learned behavior, especially if we grew up being taught that our reality is somehow less than.

The solution is to have strong boundaries, and these come from being crystal clear about your values and principles independent of what other people say and want. How do you nail down your values? While you can do this work with a friend or therapist, the truth is that only you can decide what matters to you!

If this an area you struggle with, write down a few answers to these questions (and don't share them!):

- Who do you most admire, and why? What characteristics do they demonstrate?
- Think about past experiences where you felt deeply fulfilled and good about yourself. What was it about these experiences that made them mean so much to you?
- What do you consider the *worst* behavior possible, or something truly unforgivable that you would never, ever do (this hints at the opposite of your values!)
- What things mattered most to you when you were a little child? (i.e., before other people told you what to focus on)
- Consider the last big decision you made. What made you choose as you did?
- When have you been most disappointed in yourself, and why?

- What would you focus on in life if nobody else's opinion mattered?
- On your deathbed, what kinds of events, choices, and themes do you imagine you'd most dwell on?

Answering these questions will help you identify what matters most to you. Do you value kindness and compassion? Do you consider the purpose of life to learn and evolve? Do you think family is more important than anything? Would you fight to the death for the rights of the innocent? Is your ultimate goal to find material and financial security in life? Are you a romantic who cares about love, beauty, and pleasure? Do you think you're put here on this earth to express yourself and create new things? Is your primary mission to be an independent and open-minded freethinker? Or do you think that dependability, loyalty, and service are the keys to happiness?

Whatever they are, your values will give your life color, direction, focus, and purpose. They will strengthen you in the face of conflict and guide you in times of confusion. Tuning into your values gives you an internal locus of control, so you see yourself as the conscious agent in your life rather than assuming that other people know better and will steer your life for you. True, you may still experience conflict and difference with other people, but if you have truly identified your deepest values, then you will not feel that difference or disagreement as a threat—you will stay strong in your convictions and express yourself whether people approve or not.

Even if you're not one hundred percent sure about your values yet (and yes, they can change!), you can still practice standing your ground and being self-differentiated by regularly distinguishing between your stuff and the other person's. Having the courage to be yourself may look as extreme as ending relationships that don't serve you anymore, or as trivial as refusing to change your opinion just because it's not popular.

Values will help you refine your boundaries to decide what is and isn't acceptable to you. A fun way to give your boundaries a tune up is to compose your own list of ten "life rules." Write down your personal manifesto, putting down ten rules that speak to your values; for example, "I will never lie" and "I strive to make people's lives better."

Look at your list and convert each rule into a boundary when you're done. For example, "I do not tolerate other people lying to me," or, "I do not get into relationships that diminish me and make my life worse." Remember that a boundary is always a rule about how *you* will behave—it's not a prescription for other people. Clarify your own values, and your boundaries naturally flow from that conviction.

Working with Your Inner Child

The final obstacle is allowing unhealthy habits and patterns from the past to dominate the present. Knowing your triggers and pain points can help you heal them instead of letting your past determine your present and future. This means switching from passive and reactive to conscious and proactive. Remember that when you are triggered, you have two options: you can react to the trigger itself, or you can step back and ask where that trigger is coming from. As in our above example, you can start fighting with the person who you fear is abandoning you, or you can look within and explore the causes of your fear of abandonment.

If you simply react, the trigger is only reinforced and the habit strengthened. But if you question and challenge your knee-jerk reactions, you give yourself the chance to update and try something different— something better. You'll know that you're in the grip of ingrained unhealthy habits when you can recognize yourself behaving in maladaptive ways yet can't seem to stop yourself. Poor mental health, destructive coping mechanisms (for example, substance abuse), high reactivity, or repeating the same relationship patterns repeatedly are all signs you could use some "reprogramming" at the childhood level.

Here's a technique for doing what's commonly called "inner child work," although each therapist will have different approaches. Use whatever method you like best for entering a relaxed and meditative state; for example, deep breathing, visualization, or mantras. Spend some time alone trying to recall the first time you encountered a particular emotion in your mind's eye. For example, you might want to get to the root of your fear of abandonment. Perhaps a memory of being literally abandoned as a child pops into your mind?

Next, flesh out a mental image of yourself as a young child. Let that child just be what they are and feel what they feel without judgment or resistance. Watch that child from the present as the adult you are now. Perhaps you see them as small, frightened, alone. Approach this child and have a conversation. What does the child say? What do they want? What are they concerned about? What do they feel and why?

This takes a little creativity, an open mind, and a willingness to let your unconscious self guide you for a while. Imagine that you are talking to this inner child who is, in fact, a version of yourself. Don't approach with any agenda, but simply become curious about what it's like to be them. Most of all, be curious about their *needs*.

The magic of this technique happens when you essentially "reparent" your younger self from the more conscious, more mature vantage point in the present. For example, you might see your younger self in a memory where you were lost in a shopping mall, terrified to the core and vulnerable. You talk to this child and discover that they have a deep need to feel safe and cared for and protected. Back then, this need wasn't met. And you may have developed a range of reactions, habits, coping mechanisms, and even defenses to help deal with this unmet need.

As the adult, you approach your inner child and directly meet this need for them.

In our example, you might imagine a scene where you comfort this child, help them find their way home, or encourage them to be brave. You might hug and kiss them, tell them they're awesome, or simply listen to them. Whatever they need, you as the adult can supply it to you as the child. There may be something profoundly healing in the realization that *you will never abandon yourself,* and that no matter what happens, you will always be there to validate, protect, and care for yourself.

A simpler way of doing this exercise is to ask:

What did your younger self most need to hear then?
And what did they most need to say and have others hear?

Now, as an adult, you have the power to tell your younger self what they needed to hear ("It's not your fault!"), and listen to them in the way they needed ("nobody listened to you back then, but I'm listening now . . ."). None of us can go back into the past and change it, but we can give ourselves what we need right now.

Did you need to be listened to and taken seriously? Then listen to yourself right now. Did you need adults to protect you better? Commit to treating yourself as a precious thing to be protected in the present. Did you need more love and affection? Then love yourself as much as you need right now.

Did you need to be told that you were good and lovable just as you were? That is now your job—make a promise to yourself to never judge and criticize that inner child again, but to give them the love they need.

Another relatively easy way to practice this is to get very familiar with your triggers, and work with them rather than reacting to them. For example, if you always get stressed and angry when you visit your parents over Christmas, notice what triggers the feelings. Maybe it's being dismissed, interrupted, or talked over. Now, instead of going to war with the trigger itself (i.e., being reactive) become curious about why the trigger is there and what you can do to meet your needs in that moment. You can combine this with the "I feel X because I need Y" format.

Trigger: Mom talking over me.
Emotion: Anger.
Unmet need: To be recognized as an autonomous adult, to be respected as an equal in the family.
How to meet this need myself: I can calmly assert my boundaries. "Mom, when you

interrupt me, I feel really angry and upset because I need to be spoken to like an adult. I love you and want to enjoy our conversations. Can you not interrupt me when I speak?" If Mom continues to disrespect this boundary, I won't go to blame. Instead, I can meet my own need to be an autonomous adult and simply leave!

Inner child work can be long, delicate, and vulnerable work. But if you get it right, you release yourself from the stale old patterns and traps from the past and fully inhabit the present. This means you are more available to genuinely and spontaneously connect with people. You are no longer playing out tired scripts from a story that ended long ago. Without projections, blame, shame, self-doubt, passivity, or unresolved trauma, you are simply who you are—real, vibrantly alive, and authentic. And when you function this way, you cannot help but have fulfilling, mature, meaningful, and respectful connections with others. When the obstacles are removed, a healthy connection to others is easy, immediate, and natural—it's what you were born to do!

Takeaways:

- Whether we know it or not, the purpose of all communication is to meet our needs. We can become better communicators (and improve our relationships) if we learn to properly understand, take responsibility for, and meet our own needs before we approach others. We can also improve communication by learning to proactively meet our own needs.
- We can take steps to minimize or remove the obstacles standing in the way of effective communication.
- Obstacle 1 is not knowing ourselves and projecting our own issues or unmet needs onto other people, causing conflict. We can address this by noticing when we have a strong, automatic reaction or resistance, and becoming curious about it rather than reactivity.
- Obstacle 2 is a VERB mindset—playing victim, acting entitled, awaiting rescue, or blaming others. A healthier mindset is based on taking responsibility for our own thoughts, feelings, and experiences.

We can do this by first noticing feelings, asking what unmet needs create that feeling, and then exploring ways to meet this need ourselves.

- Obstacle 3 is a lack of self-differentiation and needing others to tell you what to think or feel. You can strengthen this area by discovering your own deeply held values. Knowing your values gives you courage and conviction, and clarity in how to act, despite other people's choices.

- The final obstacle is getting stuck in old patterns and habitual behaviors stemming from childhood. We can reparent our inner child, listening to what they needed to say back then, and telling them what they needed to hear. We can give ourselves what we needed as children, thus releasing the coping mechanisms we developed to deal with unmet needs in the past.

- By working with triggers rather than reacting to them, we release old habits and can be more authentic, spontaneous, and present in our relationships right now.

Summary Guide

CHAPTER 1: THE BIGGEST OBSTACLE TO REAL COMMUNICATION

- Everyone can learn to be better at communication, listening, and being heard. This can improve every kind of relationship and help you deal with difficult people and conflict.
- Cultivating empathetic, meaningful, and genuine connections with others means being aware of the barriers to that connection and committing to removing them.
- One significant obstacle is the mindset that positions others as enemies or adversaries rather than collaborators on the same team. A healthier approach is "it's you and me versus the problem." Disagreement and difference are not

necessarily a threat if both parties are dedicated to working together.

- Assume noble intent and that people are doing their best. This will put you in a proactive, generous, and optimistic frame of mind that will inspire the best from others and keep you open to solutions and possibilities. Be kind and seek the moral high ground just because!

- In conflict, try to imagine a neutral observer and the "third story" they'd tell so you can identify a set of facts about the situation that both parties can agree on. Harmonious relationships begin when we abandon our egoistic need to be right.

- In every interaction, consciously address the other person's highest self, or at least their most vulnerable and human self. Acknowledge emotional content and not just superficial details. Have compassion, awareness, and genuine curiosity for other people's different perspectives.

- Finally, master self-differentiation and be crystal clear on thoughts versus feelings, and your thoughts and feelings versus those of others. Defuse conflict by taking responsibility for your perspective while seeing the other person's for what it is. Most important, have the maturity to maintain intimacy with others despite differences in opinion. Routinely ask what your "business" versus theirs is and what is observation versus evaluation.

CHAPTER 2: REAL-WORLD SKILLS FOR BETTER COMMUNICATION

- Better communication skills stem from a healthy mindset and a good attitude toward relationships in general.
- We can practice and communicate self-differentiation by knowing and taking responsibility for communicating our own needs. Then we can establish boundaries and gently but firmly assert them. Boundaries are not rules for others' behavior, but ours.
- Empathy is the ability to understand and feel into someone else's experience, and take action to help them. There are three types—cognitive, emotional, and compassionate.

- First, gain cognitive empathy by switching perspectives, listening, asking questions, and seeking to understand. Next, find emotional empathy by addressing their higher natures and assuming the best of them, or find common ground. Finally, offer compassionate empathy by taking action to enhance their wellbeing.

- We stay open-minded and humble with curiosity and approach others in a spirit of opportunity, respect, and the desire to learn. Express genuine interest in someone by asking open-ended questions and listening to the answers. Don't assume, let people speak, and check your comprehension by paraphrasing.

- Humility is the virtue that will allow you to quickly and sincerely own up to mistakes. This takes courage and maturity. Make sure any apologies show remorse, repentance, and full responsibility, as well as explain what went wrong, what you will do to fix it, and a request for forgiveness. Accept any response to your apology with grace.

- Practice conversational patience, listen to others, and give them the space to be as they are. Cut out the ego!
- You can validate others by asking questions every time you're tempted to jump in and hog attention. Relax, slow down, and have the self-discipline and compassion to let the conversation unfolds as it will, rather than as you think it should.

CHAPTER 3: WHAT TO SAY AND HOW TO SAY IT

- In the Imago framework, we seek to remove emotional barriers to connection by communicating. The Sender and the Receiver take turns sharing their message.
- The Receiver listens by mirroring, validating, and communicating empathy as the Sender speaks. Then, they change places. The key is to be patient, not interrupt, and avoid trying to be the Sender when acting as the Receiver.

- Active listening techniques help us absorb, understand, remember, and respond to what we're told. This includes non-judgment, reflection, paying attention, seeking clarification, summarizing, and possibly sharing your own experience.
- It's important to avoid using language that triggers defensiveness. This includes things like "what's wrong with you?" "I'm sorry you feel that way," "whatever," "you're overreacting," "you're entitled to your opinion," or anything using absolute terms like "always" and "never." These are invalidating and inflammatory and will be met with resistance, emphasizing emotional barriers rather than dissolving them.
- Immersing yourself in someone else's equally valid reality is harder than it looks, and so we need to routinely test our assumptions. We need to ask people questions and challenge our assumptions about what they think or feel or how we attribute their actions.
- Psychologizing people is a way we can believe we're listening compassionately,

but actually, we're forcing our interpretation or worldview onto another person instead of genuinely listening to their experience.

- The four principles of Marshall Rosenberg's non-violent communication are: observations, feelings, needs, and requests, in that order.
- First, make neutral observations instead of judgmental evaluations. Next, seek to explore feelings and not opinions. Be careful about using "you" statements or attributing blame, and instead take responsibility for your own experience. Next, connect your feelings with any unmet needs with the format: "I feel X because I need Y." Finally, end with a respectful and reasonable request focused on your needs.

CHAPTER 4: HOW TO OWN YOUR EMOTIONS

- Whether we know it or not, the purpose of all communication is to meet our needs. We can become better communicators (and improve our relationships) if we learn to properly understand, take responsibility for, and meet our own needs before we approach others. We can also improve communication by learning to proactively meet our own needs.

- We can try to minimize or remove the obstacles standing in the way of effective communication.

- Obstacle 1 is not knowing ourselves and projecting our issues or unmet needs onto other people, causing conflict. We can address this by noticing when we have a strong, automatic reaction or resistance, and becoming curious about it rather than reactivity.

- Obstacle 2 is a VERB mindset—playing victim, acting entitled, awaiting rescue, or blaming others. A healthier mindset is based on taking responsibility for our own thoughts, feelings, and experiences. We can do this by first noticing feelings, asking what unmet needs create that feeling, and then exploring ways to meet this need ourselves.

- Obstacle 3 is a lack of self-differentiation and needing others to tell you what to think or feel. You can strengthen this area by discovering your own deeply held values. Knowing your values gives you courage and conviction and clarity in how to act, despite other people's choices.

- The final obstacle is getting stuck in old patterns and habitual behaviors stemming from childhood. We can reparent our inner child, listening to what they needed to say back then, and telling them what they needed to hear. We can give ourselves what we needed as children, thus releasing the coping mechanisms we developed to deal with unmet needs in the past.

- By working with triggers rather than reacting to them, we release old habits and can be more authentic, spontaneous, and present in our relationships right now.

Printed in Great Britain
by Amazon

14813920R00098